God's Call Is Everywhere

A Global Analysis of Contemporary Religious Vocations for Women

Patricia Wittberg, SC
Mary L. Gautier
Gemma Simmonds, CJ
with Nathalie Becquart, XMCJ

Foreword by Patricia Murray, IBVM

**LITURGICAL PRESS
ACADEMIC**

Collegeville, Minnesota
www.litpress.org

Cover art courtesy of Adobe Stock.

© 2023 by Patricia Wittberg, SC, Mary L. Gautier, Gemma Simmonds, CJ, Nathalie Becquart, XMCJ

Published by Liturgical Press, Collegeville, Minnesota. All rights reserved. No part of this book may be used or reproduced in any manner whatsoever, except brief quotations in reviews, without written permission of Liturgical Press, Saint John's Abbey, PO Box 7500, Collegeville, MN 56321-7500. Printed in the United States of America.

1   2   3   4   5   6   7   8   9

Library of Congress Cataloging-in-Publication Data

Names: Wittberg, Patricia, 1947– author.
Title: God's call is everywhere : a global analysis of contemporary religious vocations for women / Patricia Wittberg, SC, Mary L. Gautier, Gemma Simmonds, CJ with, Nathalie Becquart, XMCJ ; foreword by Patricia Murray, IBVM.
Description: Collegeville, Minnesota : Liturgical Press Academic, [2023] | Includes bibliographical references and index. | Summary: "God's Call Is Everywhere is a comparative analysis of research in six countries investigating women who have entered vowed religious life in Catholicism in the twenty-first century. The data include survey responses from institute leaders, formation directors, and the women themselves, conducted in the United States, Canada, Australia, and France, along with focus groups and interviews in Ireland, the United Kingdom, and France. By examining a summary of these studies and comparing differences, readers will have a better understanding of the hopes and concerns of those discerning a vocation to religious life and learn how to move forward in the future"— Provided by publisher.
Identifiers: LCCN 2023015985 (print) | LCCN 2023015986 (ebook) | ISBN 9780814669136 (paperback) | ISBN 9780814669143 (epub) | ISBN 9780814669150 (pdf)
Subjects: LCSH: Monasticism and religious orders for women. | Vocation—Catholic Church. | Vocation, Ecclesiastical.
Classification: LCC BX4210 .W57 2023 (print) | LCC BX4210 (ebook) | DDC 255/.9—dc23/eng/20230622
LC record available at https://lccn.loc.gov/2023015985
LC ebook record available at https://lccn.loc.gov/2023015986

"Instead of the typical focus on diminishment and aging of women religious, this book gives a hopeful outlook by focusing on what is present and the joy and hope held by those who are still hearing God's call. It should be required reading for all who are involved in the administration of women's religious institutes and the formation of newer religious."

—Juliet Mousseau, author of *Prophetic Witnesses to Joy*

"The National Religious Vocation Conference (NRVC) is grateful for the inclusion of two of its major studies in this new book as it noticeably recognizes the global impact of our mission. The NRVC endorses this book and its contributors as it broadens the key messages about the women and men who have entered religious life since 1993. As God continues to call, the NRVC research in this book amplifies the response of newer entrants who have abundant hope amid changing demographics."

—Deborah M. Borneman, SSCM, National Religious Vocation Conference Director of Mission Integration

"*God's Call Is Everywhere* should be recommended reading for anyone involved in vocational ministry. It truly is a snapshot of the current generation of young women who are discerning and developing their response to the call of God. While there is a decrease in women choosing religious life, this book clearly indicates that God is still calling. However, it is a noisy world with many distractions, and it can be hard to find suitable people to 'walk together' on the path of discernment."

—Gerard Gallagher, Communications and Membership Services, Association of Leaders of Missionaries and Religious of Ireland

"God's call is indeed everywhere, and we can learn from how it is manifested in the lives of young women all over the world! This book offers a big picture understanding of women's religious life through the qualitative study of the words of its newest and youngest members. The true benefit of this book is the insights gained from considering a global experience of the gifts and challenges of religious life today as experienced by its newest members. Knowledge of global perspectives offers opportunities to consider how religious life as we know it is consistent with the rest of the world. Understanding challenges faced elsewhere helps us grapple with our own complex local contexts as we seek to share the gifts of religious life with the next generations."

— Sarah Kohles, OSF, editor of *In Our Own Words: Religious Life in a Changing World*

Contents

Foreword *by Patricia Murray, IBVM* vii

List of Tables and Figures xvii

List of Contributors xxi

Chapter 1 Introduction 1

Chapter 2 Comparing Institutes of Women Religious and Their Newer Members 9

Chapter 3 Generational Differences among Newer Entrants to Religious Life 41

Chapter 4 Obstacles to Vocation Discernment and Entrance 79

Chapter 5 New Vocations and Vocational Exploration in Britain and Ireland 103

Chapter 6 Women's Religious Life Vocations in Mexico: Elements for Further Reflection 139

Chapter 7 Vocation to Religious Life: Through the Lens of Young Religious in India 151

Chapter 8 Experiences of Newer Religious Vocations in Kenya 167

Chapter 9 Reflection on Religious Life and the Future Challenges, Opportunities, and Dreams 183

Chapter 10   Formation Implications from the Data
             for Religious Life's Newest Members   193

Chapter 11   Conclusion   203

References   211

Index   217

Foreword

Every so often a book is published on a particular topic that is essential reading. This is how I view *God's Call Is Everywhere: A Global Analysis of Contemporary Religious Vocations for Women*. This is a masterful study because it provides both sociological data together with theological and experiential insights to facilitate reflection on how newer members view contemporary religious life in various parts of the world. The study begins by focusing on data gathered from these newer members from the United States, Australia, Canada, Ireland, France, and the United Kingdom. Some comparative perspectives are then offered from other parts of the world—Mexico, India, and Kenya—and from different generational perspectives. These latter serve as further interpretative keys to reflect on the data provided. Pre– and post–Vatican II Generations, Generations X, Y, and Z have all had very different life experiences and experiences of religious life. Clearly intergenerational dialogue can offer insights and perspectives when determining the essentials of religious life. Finally, the remaining chapters reflect the perspective of formation and vocation promotion.

This book is essential reading for every member of a religious institute, particularly for congregational leaders and those responsible for formation programs, because it provides important materials for personal and communal reflection. It will also interest those who engage in academic studies on female religious life. We know that it is important to keep reading "the signs of the times" to engage in ongoing discernment with regard to imagining the way forward for consecrated life. We particularly need to read "the signs of the times" as described by those who are becoming new members of congregations today. How they are experiencing and responding to the call to religious life will differ from those who have been members for many decades.

The context in which women discern a vocation to religious life has changed radically, both locally and globally. We need to remember that, according to Pope Francis, "we are not living an era of change but a change of eras." The document *New Wine in New Wineskins*, published by the Vatican Dicastery for Institutes of Consecrated Life and Societies of Apostolic Life in 2017, says in paragraph 9 that using the metaphor of new wine, "we can ask ourselves if what we are savoring and offering to drink is actually *new wine* that is full-bodied and wholesome." *God's Call Is Everywhere: A Global Analysis of Contemporary Religious Vocations for Women* provides us with the means to undertake reflection in depth. The *New Wine in New Wineskins* document notes in paragraph 13 that what is important is "not the preservation of forms; it is the willingness, in creative continuity, to re-think the consecrated life as the evangelical memory of a permanent state of conversion from which intuitions and concrete choices flow." The various chapters in this book demonstrate the willingness to reexamine consecrated life as it evolves and is being reshaped within the creative continuity to which the document refers.

We are living at a time when we are experiencing increased secularization with the process of globalization. In addition, as we experience the de-westernization or the de-Europeanization of religious life it is important to examine the impact of these developments on religious life in different parts of the world. It is clear that change is occurring within female religious life in relation to the number of vocations. Recent statistics issued by the Vatican indicate that the total number of religious women in the world at the end of 2021 was 608,958, a decrease of

1.7% from 619,546 at the end of 2020. This is a far cry from the days when there were over 1 million religious women. Yet, as we read in the initial chapter presenting an historical overview of consecrated life, there have always been periods of decline and growth if we look at patterns purely from a numerical perspective. It has been precisely during these times of diminution that the seeds of the new have been sown, which have led to a new understanding of the meaning and purpose of religious life and the emergence of new forms or new emphases.

During the current synodal journey with its emphasis on walking together, we have been reminded that, in a spirit of radical inclusion, we need to hear all the voices and to make a special option for including the voices of younger people. Therefore, reading the outcomes of surveys, focus groups, and interviews provides a way of entering into the experience of younger women who have joined religious life more recently in the United States, Australia, Canada, Ireland, France, and the United Kingdom. These countries are increasingly secular in outlook and therefore joining a religious congregation is often seen by younger people to be countercultural. These newer members join congregations that are largely comprised of an aging membership which is gradually being replaced by a much smaller, and more culturally diverse, younger membership. The data presented emphasizes one of the challenges highlighted in *New Wine in New Wineskins* where it refers to the experience of some newer members who "have found themselves in a situation that is hard to manage: on one side, a few dozen elderly members, who are tied to the classic, and sometimes altered, cultural and institutional traditions, and on the other, a large number of young members from different cultures who tremble, who feel marginalized, and who no longer accept subordinate roles" (paragraph 13).

Each chapter offers different windows on the experience of those discerning and entering religious life. Key areas of importance emerge in relation to those who have discerned a vocation to religious life and have responded to God's call. These include the importance of prayer, of living an authentic community life, and of making visible the charism and mission of the congregation. The responses show that the ministries of the congregation are seen to be a less significant part of the discernment. It is important to note the similarities and differences which are found across the responses from different parts of the world. Factors such as nationality or ethnicity and social class do influence whether women are attracted to religious life and the type of religious institute that they are likely to join as well as their hopes and expectations in relation to their vocation. Where theological and ecclesiological differences exist within the local church, these are replicated across the choice of religious congregations.

Personal contact clearly plays a vitally important part in any discernment of a religious vocation. The first contacts with a religious institute generally come through meeting with or working with a member of the congregation or through a recommendation from a friend or spiritual director or perhaps through meeting congregational members at an event. Print materials, websites, social media, and even vocational stories are generally seen to be much less impactful. Receiving encouragement and feeling welcomed during the discernment process and after entering the congregation are important experiences. When asked to evaluate their institutes, participants described them as excellent in terms of instilling a sense of identity, fidelity to the Church and its teaching, fostering mission, and responding to the needs of the times. However, efforts to promote social justice were seen to be less vibrant. The different surveys provide the reader with a wealth of experiential data from new members, and valuable material on which we can all reflect.

The generational study across Australia, Canada, France, Ireland, the United Kingdom, and the United States uses quantitative and qualitative measures—surveys, open-ended questions, interviews, and focus groups—to offer many important insights in relation to a wide variety of topics. These include how religious women name their hopes and concerns about the future, the loss/growth in personal/community identity, religious fervor, the loss/growth in holiness, prayer and community life, fidelity to the vows/charism, openness to change, preservation of the traditional model of religious life, mission and ministry, opportunities for personal growth and development. While the questions posed and the methodology used varied from country to country, many of the topics emerging overlap, while those that differ provide key insights into topics of importance in particular parts of the world. The extensive list of sample responses offers a rich source for further reflection and discussion on many different aspects of consecrated life. As we read these, many responses and reflections they have may echo or diverge from our own experience of consecrated life. However, they highlight the diversity of perspectives which in turn invite us to deep listening and to finding ways of creating unity, in the middle of what Sr. Marie Chin, RSM, has described elsewhere, as "luxurious diversity."

Obstacles to vocation discernment and entrance are many, with significant differences in various parts of the world. General cultural factors, attitudes about the Church, the discerner's background, family, and life within the institutes themselves all play a part in encouraging or discouraging a religious vocation. Within institutes issues such as age difference, the quality of formation, apathy among current members, and the absence of vibrant communities are identified as factors affecting discernment and retention. For those discerning religious life, a fear of commitment, immaturity, dysfunctional family life, individualism, and an overidealized vision of religious life are seen as further obstacles to discernment. Again and again, it is emphasized that community members need to be able to adapt to welcome new members coming from changed contexts. In addition, members need to be well prepared to have the necessary skills to accompany discerners.

A qualitative study, focused on the UK and Ireland, looks at new vocations and vocational exploration. It affirms that women continue to hear and respond to God's call and that they are attracted by the witness of coherent commitment, prayer, community life, charism, and mission. Increasingly they are finding creative ways to deal with cultural and generational differences and to demonstrate a strong commitment to live in solidarity with those on the margins. Clearly, structures and the internal culture of religious life need to change if those seeking to enter are to be accommodated and to find a healthy way of life within communities. If the life is to survive and flourish, religious need above all to understand and adapt to today's cultural context.

Comparisons with religious life in locations in the global South are particularly helpful. The experience in Mexico raises questions about material and psychological distancing between consecrated and ordinary life. Images of fortress, drawbridge, and an enclosure with narrow skylights depict consecrated life as one detached from an ordinary manner of life. The *Latinobarómetro* study asked newer entrants to religious institutes the following simple question: *When you came to live with us or when you met us, what were the practices of life (customs, ways of living, routines) that were most difficult for you to understand and live?* Their responses show that many institutional beliefs and practices no longer have meaning or relevance for younger members. The requirement to get permission for everything, to follow an overly structured routine, to give up wearing the clothes a person is used to wearing or a mobile phone is met with incomprehension. Consecrated life is often seen to be enclosed in its own world, blaming the newer members for any dysfunctionality rather than undertaking a serious discernment on how to adapt to changing times. However, these younger religious value their religious life and offer many strategies for improvement.

Vocations in India are declining, mirroring what has already happened in the global North. Smaller families, more opportunities for women, lack of family support, and changing social values are among the reasons listed for this change. Consecrated life needs to acknowledge its internal weaknesses. One respondent notes that "instead of building communities we spend our whole energy constructing many buildings." Others decry the fact that often educational and job opportunities and ministry placements are distributed according to caste, class, friendship, family ties, and like-mindedness. This is a serious matter that urgently needs to be settled. Power, position, and personal needs are seen for some as the driving factors for women who enter religious life and stay. This calls for serious reflection on processes of accompaniment, discernment, and admission. Respondents react to being treated as workhorses and for the lack of impartiality among those in authority. There is a deep desire for authentic communion, participation, and mission based on listening and dialogue. The synodal pathway is offering a way for consecrated life to tackle necessary reforms and changes.

The experiences of new members entering religious life in Kenya echo many of the same experiences of women entering in Mexico and India. However, those who consider religious life tend to be younger and have received fewer educational opportunities than those in the global North. They begin to consider a religious vocation around the age of fifteen and enter when they have finished high school. Only 4 percent of those who enter have already received a bachelor's degree. Their reasons for entering echo those of seekers in other parts of the world—prayer and spiritual growth, outreach to the poor, and community life. Like their counterparts, they mention the difficulty of living in an overstructured community and of adapting to the internal culture of the congregation. Little connection seems to be made between the career path on which the discerner has embarked and the future ministry assigned. Many appreciate the love, care, hospitality, and concern for the individual which they experience within community. However, conflict is not seen to be managed adequately and vocational discernment is not rigorous enough to discourage those who choose religious life for the wrong reasons.

The perspective on vocational discernment in Ireland highlights the difficulty when radicality of the life and cultural hostility confront one another. While numbers may be small, the quality is perhaps stronger than ever. The desire for intimacy with God and the opportunity to live an authentic Christ-centered life still calls women to respond. Those who are seekers tend to be older, professionally qualified, and deeply spiritual. They search for a community which provides the opportunity to deepen faith through prayer, silence, and ministry. The context in Ireland presents a faith crisis rather than a vocation crisis as the Church suffers the fallout from abuses of multiple kinds. The failures of the few have become the narrative of the many and these biases need to be confronted and exposed. The journeys of vocation and synodality seem to have coalesced as seekers and believers find themselves invited to stay in the boat where Jesus is asleep, knowing that the new awakening will happen. This is a profound biblical narrative and image for reflection in many parts of the world.

The implications for formation emerge from the various components treated in this study. A focus on social justice is essential as the new entrants have generally already engaged in different social justice programs and initiatives. The absence of well-trained personnel for the ministry of formation is worrying since there are excellent programs available in different parts of the world. Unless this is tackled, formation personnel will develop programs based on their own experience rather than on the diverse life experience of those coming into religious life now. We are reminded that they are not naïve individuals or a *tabula rasa* on which information is written. Instead, quality programs must be offered either within the congregation or in inter-congregational settings that build on their experience and link theology and practice. Those entering today use a different language to describe their call and their hopes and dreams. We must listen to "the more" for which they are searching rather than imposing old models and ideas. To offer them experiences of intentional community living in larger intergenerational communities, we may have to imagine new configurations especially in international settings.

The concluding chapter brings together key insights that have emerged throughout the book. In highlighting problems and challenges, it sets out an agenda for reflection and action, particularly on the part of leaders and formators. Internal stratification based on culture, ethnicity, education, or other factors calls for in-depth cultural training in initial and ongoing formation. The aim is to learn how to create intercultural communities that can witness to unity in diversity in our fractured and broken world. Congregations also need to undertake a cultural audit to determine whether cultural experiences within communities are negative or positive. Topics such as racism and prejudice, stereotyping, and cultural generalizing need to be addressed.

The fact that currently an all-encompassing Catholic formation is increasingly rare points to the need to develop good theologically based catechesis in schools and parishes. In addition, women religious need theological training as well as good professional preparation for ministry. Today's church needs sisters as theologians, spiritual directors, economists, environmentalists, lawyers, financial and organizational managers as well as others well prepared for a wide range of educational, health, social, and pastoral ministries. Sisters need training in various methods of prayer and in discernment in order to share spiritual practices with others. Honest conversations in a spirit of contemplative dialogue need to take place between sisters of different generations to promote mutual understanding and to grow in the ability to live interculturally. Above all, in the context of the synodal journey sisters today need to be able to walk alongside others sharing how and where they see the Spirit calling the Church today.

God's Call Is Everywhere: A Global Analysis of Contemporary Religious Vocations for Women gives visibility and voice to many elements which have already surfaced in community conversations, documents on religious life, and chapter deliberations. The data and reflections presented here offer important insights from younger members. We can turn again to the guidelines from the Dicastery for Institutes of Consecrated Life and Societies of Apostolic Life, which exhort us not to be afraid of changing things according to the laws of the Gospel: "New wine requires the ability to go beyond the models we have inherited in order to appreciate the newness brought on by the Spirit, to accept it with gratitude, and to guard it, not just temporarily, but until the fermentation has finished" (*New Wine in New Wineskins*, paragraph 55). We pray that the voice and insights of younger members, together in dialogue and discernment with the wisdom and experience of others, may guide the preparation of the new wineskins needed to hold the fruit of the harvests coming from new seasons.

Sr. Patricia Murray, IBVM
Executive Secretary – International Union of Superiors
    General (UISG)
Rome, March 2023

Tables and Figures

Table 2.1 Characteristics of Institutes of Women Religious Responding to the Surveys
Table 2.2 Characteristics of Members in Institutes of Women Religious Responding to the Surveys
Table 2.3 Age and Nativity of Members in Institutes of Women Religious
Table 2.4 Characteristics of Newer Members Responding to the Surveys
Table 2.5 Education and Religious Upbringing of Newer Members
Table 2.6 Experiences of Newer Members Before Entering Religious Life
Figure 2.1 Attracted "Very Much" to religious life by . . .
Figure 2.2 Attracted "Very Much" to their institute by . . .
Figure 2.3 Attracted "Very Much" to their institute by . . .
Figure 2.4 First became acquainted with your institute through . . .
Figure 2.5 Took part in this before entering your institute
Figure 2.6 At least "Somewhat" helpful when discerning your call to religious life
Figure 2.7 Influenced "Very Much" your decision to enter your institute

Figure 2.8   Received "Very Much" encouragement when first considered entering from . . .

Figure 2.9   Currently receive "Very Much" encouragement from . . .

Figure 2.10 Currently receive "Very Much" encouragement from . . .

Figure 2.11 Types of prayer that are "Very" important to you

Figure 2.12 "Very Much" preferred composition of living setting

Figure 2.13 Institute is "Excellent" at these activities

Figure 2.14 Institute is "Excellent" at these activities

Figure 2.15 Institute is "Excellent" in these aspects

Figure 2.16 Institute is "Excellent" at these formation activities

Table 3.1   Hopes and *Concerns* about the Future, by Generation

Table 3.2   Quantitative Survey Responses (USA 2019), by Generation

Table 3.3   Hopes and *Concerns* about the Future, by Generation

Table 3.4   Hopes and *Concerns* about the Future, by Generation

Table 3.5   Quantitative Survey Responses (USA 2019), by Generation

Table 3.6   Hopes and *Concerns* about the Future, by Generation

Table 3.7   Hopes and *Concerns* about the Future, by Generation

Table 3.8   Rewarding or Satisfying about Religious Life, by Generation

Table 3.9   Challenging Aspects of Religious Life, by Generation
Table 3.10 What Attracted the Respondent to Her Institute, by Generation
Table 3.11 Rewarding or Satisfying about Religious Life, by Formation Level
Table 3.12 Challenging Aspects of Religious Life, by Formation Level
Table 3.13 What Attracted the Respondent to Her Institute, by Formation Level
Table 5.1   Entrants into Religious Communities in England and Wales 1987–2021
Table 6.1   Religious Commitment: How would you describe yourself?
Table 6.2   Age Distribution of Members of Institutes of Women Religious in Mexico
Table 6.3   New Entrants to Institutes of Women Religious in Mexico
Table 7.1   Total Numbers of Women and Men Religious in India as of 2021
Figure 8.1 Gender of Respondents
Figure 8.2 Importance of Religion to Parents
Figure 8.3 Number of Siblings
Table 8.1   What was the highest level of education you completed before you entered religious life?
Figure 8.4 Percentage of Entrants with No More Than High School Education, by Gender
Figure 8.5 Education Level of Entrants to Religious Institutes, by Country
Table 8.2   Age When First Considered a Vocation to Religious Life

Table 8.3   How much did the following attract you to religious life?

Table 8.4   How much did the following attract you to your religious institute?

Contributors

Metti Amirtham, SCC, is a sister of the Sisters of the Cross of Chavanod. She holds a PhD in systematic theology from the University of Madras, India. Currently, she is the directress of the Holy Cross Spirituality Centre (Centre for the theological and spiritual formation of women religious in India) in Yercaud, India. She teaches systematic theology at various major theological colleges and seminaries. She is fully involved in forming young religious men and women and seminarians who prepare for the priesthood, giving theological courses and facilitating motivational and counseling sessions, recollections and retreats. Being an eco-feminist thinker and writer, she has made a significant contribution toward the cause of the empowerment of women and the sustainability of nature. She regularly presents papers and publishes articles on theological and social issues that affect humanity and nature. She has published more than seventy-five research articles and six books. She has been animating her religious community in six different places. She also works at the grassroots level, empowering especially Catholic women in rural and urban parishes.

Nathalie Becquart, XMCJ, is a sister of the Xavière Sisters, Missionaries of Jesus Christ in France. She earned her master's degree from HEC Paris in 1992, with a major in entrepreneurship and studied theology and philosophy at the Centre Sèvres of Paris and sociology at the School for Advanced Studies in the Social Sciences (EHESS). Before becoming a sister, she worked as a consultant in marketing and advertising. After entering, she worked in marketing for Paulist Press, was the national coordinator for a scouting program for poor urban youth, director of a university chaplaincy program, and a member of the bishop's council of the Diocese of Nanterre, France. She played a large role in the preparation for the 2018 Synod of Bishops on young people, the faith and vocational discernment in Rome at the Vatican—as speaker, coordinator of the pre-synod, and observer at the synod. She was director of the national office for youth evangelization and vocations at the French Bishops' conference from 2012 to 2018 and was appointed a consultor to the Synod of Bishops of the Catholic Church in 2019. In February 2021, she was appointed by Pope Francis as undersecretary of the Synod of Bishops and in December 2021 was appointed a member of the Dicastery for Communication. Her most recent book is *The Spirit Renews Everything* (Paris: Salvator Press, 2020).

Margaret Cartwright is married, with three daughters and four grandchildren. Margaret has a BA in theology and spirituality, MA in pastoral leadership, and MA in supervisory practice. She has also completed the two-year spiritual director's course with the Jesuits in Manresa. Margaret has held positions in parish ministry and in lay ministry training, both in Ireland and Papua New Guinea. She was a supervisor of BA and MA pastoral students in All Hallows College, Dublin. Margaret held the role of director of health care chaplaincy in Mount Carmel Hospital, Dublin, and served for six years on the Healthcare Chaplaincy Board. Margaret is currently director of Vocations Ireland and has held this role for seven years, including six years on the National Vocation Council in Maynooth. Margaret also serves as an international coordinator with the National Religious Vocation Conference (NRVC) in Chicago. Vocations Ireland is an office within the Association of Leaders of Missionaries and Religious of Ireland.

Ellen Dauwer, SC, is a sister of the Sisters of Charity of Saint Elizabeth. She most recently served as executive director of the Religious Formation Conference, based at Catholic Theological Union in Chicago. Prior to that, she served in congregational leadership for two terms. Most of her ministry has been in the field of education: as a high school math and computer science teacher, as a college professor in Computer Information Systems and Educational Technology, and as a college administrator at both the College of Saint Elizabeth in New Jersey and Fordham University in New York. She also spent a year as a fellow of the American Council on Education (program in leadership in higher education). Sr. Ellen holds a BA in education and math from the College of Saint Elizabeth, an MA in measurement and evaluation and a PhD in management of computer resources (both from New York University).

Luis Fernando Falcó, MSpS, is a Mexican priest and member of the Missionaries of the Holy Spirit congregation. He trained as a psychotherapist and psychoanalyst (1995–2001) at the Asociación Psicoanalítica Jalisciense, in Guadalajara, México, and completed doctoral studies in political science and sociology at UNAM (Universidad Nacional Autónoma de México; 2013–2017). Fr. Falcó served in religious formation ministry for twenty-one years in his congregation and was rector of the Instituto de Formación Filosófica Intercongregacional de México, an inter-congregational initiative of philosophical formation for religious. He has been director of Proyecto Cruces since its foundation in 2014. His professional service at Project Cruces is about formation and consultancy to religious communities and priesthood, applying organizational and psychosocial knowledge to religious life. He has written a book, *Contingencia y llamado eterno* (2010), reflecting on the new sociocultural conditions of new vocations in religious life. He currently collaborates on the

"International Research on Women Religious Life" project with CARA at Georgetown and CERRA at Kenya, coordinating the team in Mexico; he also coordinates the team of the "Oficina de Desarrollo y Salud Integral de las Religiosas en México," a project sponsored by the Hilton Foundation and monitored by CARA.

Mary L. Gautier retired in 2019 as senior research associate at CARA, the Center for Applied Research in the Apostolate at Georgetown University, a position she held for twenty-one years. Mary holds an MA and PhD in sociology from Louisiana State University. Before coming to CARA, Mary taught sociology at Louisiana State University and at Texas Christian University and served as a lay pastoral associate in Baton Rouge, Louisiana, for six years. At CARA, Mary specialized in Catholic demographic trends in the United States, managed CARA databases, and conducted demographic projects and computer-aided mapping. She also edited *The CARA Report*, a quarterly research publication, and other CARA publications. She is coauthor of twelve books on Catholicism in the United States, most recently *Migration for Mission: International Catholic Sisters in the United States* (Oxford University Press, 2019). She currently serves on the board of advisors for Liturgical Press and on the board of directors for ASEC, the African Sisters Education Collaborative.

Bibiana Ngundo, LSOSF, is a sister of the Little Sisters of St. Francis congregation. She is Kenyan and holds a PhD in religious studies from the Catholic University of Eastern Africa, Nairobi, Kenya. She is a senior lecturer in the department of religious studies, where she worked as department head for six years and currently serves as the university's coordinator of academic linkages. In addition to teaching and administrative responsibilities, she is passionate about research. In 2017, she spent six months at the Center for Applied Research in the Apostolate (CARA) in Washington, DC, learning applied research skills. Since then, she not only teaches research at the university but also works at the CERRA Data Center in Nairobi housed at the Catholic University of Eastern Africa, a project of the Hilton Foundation. At the Center, she is a member of the Research Advisory Committee. With her experience, she has led the designing, expediting, completion, and dissemination of findings of several surveys. She has authored numerous articles and book chapters as well as two books.

Gemma Simmonds, CJ, is a sister of the Congregation of Jesus. She is a senior research fellow at the Margaret Beaufort Institute of Theology in Cambridge, UK, where she is director of the Religious Life Institute, teaching Christian spirituality and pastoral theology. An international speaker and lecturer, she is an honorary fellow of Durham University, past president of the Catholic Theological Association of Great Britain, and chair of trustees of the ecumenical Community of St. Anselm based at Lambeth Palace, London. She lectured in theology at Heythrop College, University of London, specializing in spiritual direction in the Ignatian tradition, and has been a spiritual director and retreat giver for over thirty years. Gemma has been a missionary in Brazil, a chaplain in the Universities of Cambridge and London, and a chaplaincy volunteer in Holloway Prison for twenty-five years. She is a regular broadcaster on religious matters on the BBC, Radio Maria England, and other radio and television networks. Her most recent publication is *Dancing at the Still Point: Retreat Practices for Busy Lives* (London: SPCK, 2021).

Patricia Wittberg, SC, is a sister of the Sisters of Charity of Cincinnati, Ohio. She holds a PhD in sociology from the University of Chicago, is emeritus professor at Indiana University-Purdue University Indianapolis (IUPUI), and is currently a research associate with the Center for Applied

Research in the Apostolate (CARA). She is particularly interested in generational continuity and change among Catholics. Her academic research focuses on the sociology of religion, community, and church and nonprofit organizations. She is the author of numerous books and articles on Catholicism and Catholic religious life, most recently chapters in *Migration for Mission: International Catholic Sisters in the United States* (Oxford University Press, 2019) and *Faith and Spiritual Life of Young Adult Catholics in a Rising Hispanic Church* (Liturgical Press, 2022).

1

Introduction

Why should the Catholic Church—or any variety of Christianity—contain groups or individuals who are "consecrated" in some way to follow a "religious life"? This question has been asked several times throughout the millennia of the Catholicism's history. Critics have argued that Jesus did not call some of his disciples to a separate, elite religious caste—the Sermon on the Mount was directed to *all* of them (Rausch 1990:33). There were also no vowed religious for the first several centuries in the early Church. These arguments led the Protestant Reformers of the sixteenth century and later to eliminate separate religious orders from the models of Christianity they established:

> First, [Luther] argued that monastic vows suggested a superior way of life, different from that of ordinary Christians, and so were contrary to the Word of God. Second, he saw monastic life itself as an effort to justify oneself before God, and hence, contrary to his doctrine of justification by faith alone. Third, he felt that the vows were contrary to Christian liberty (Rausch 1990:84).

In the mid-twentieth century, the seminal document of Catholicism's Second Vatican Council, *Lumen Gentium*, decreed that *all* members of the Church were equally called to holiness, and not just the members of religious orders (Clarke 1986; O'Donnell 1994). So why bother having a separate "religious life" at all?

But even if theology and ecclesiology may recommend the equality of all believers as the ideal state for the People of God, or even if secular culture may look askance at the kind of spiritual hierarchy implied by having a separate, consecrated class of religious virtuosi, women and men still continue to join religious institutes today. In fact, we would argue, religious "institutes" or "orders" are essential for the Church's health and very survival. This is because they perform several important roles for the Church. First, they provide a place within the Church for those who desire to practice their faith more intensely or via a different set of spiritual practices (charismatic prayer forms, for example, or street corner preaching) than other lay Catholics. If no outlet is provided within Catholicism for their vocational calling, they will go elsewhere. This is, in fact, the pattern that has occurred several times within the history of Protestantism, precisely because it provided no recognized form of religious life. The Lutherans and Calvinists of the Reformation, for example, soon found themselves confronted by entire groups of religious enthusiasts—the Hutterites, Mennonites, and Spiritualists—for whom the established Reformation churches did not provide a sufficiently radical following of Christ (Wittberg 1996:24; Finke and Wittberg 2000). In nineteenth-century England and the United States, the Anglicans/Episcopalians found themselves eclipsed by "upstart sects" like the Methodists and Baptists (Finke and Stark 1992). Each time, their most devout members were the ones who were attracted to the new churches, impoverishing the church they had left. By keeping its religious virtuosi within its fold, Catholicism has usually (although not always) avoided this fate (Finke and Wittberg 2000).

A second essential role which religious orders have played in Catholicism is to serve as creative spiritual laboratories, adapting the Church's rituals and practices in response to changes in the larger society. Thus, the mendicant orders of the thirteenth century invented new forms and topics of preaching that spoke to the growing urban merchant class. They dominated the faculty of the new medieval universities, hammering out a theology of money-making, profit, and interest—practices which the Church had considered sinful in previous centuries (Little 1978:176–78). They also added new elements to popular devotion: the Dominican St. Thomas Aquinas, for example, wrote poems (*Pange Lingua, Adoro Te Devote, Lauda Sion*) which, set to music, are still sung today. St. Francis, it is said, erected the first Christmas crib to teach the story of Jesus's nativity to the uncatechized poor. Medieval nuns developed and popularized a model and a vocabulary for religious mystical experience, and were instrumental in obtaining popular acceptance of the Real Presence of Christ in the Eucharist (Finke and Wittberg 2000:163). In the sixteenth century, St. Ignatius of Loyola and the Jesuits developed the idea of the religious retreat using the Spiritual Exercises. Seventeenth-century religious orders of English and French women pioneered the ministry of education for young girls, which had hitherto not been considered a suitable work for their sex, to counteract the attractiveness of Protestantism (Rapley 1990:6).

The theological and devotional creativity of religious orders was also important in evangelization, by helping render Catholicism attractive to different societal groups that may have been alienated from it before and by spreading the Gospel to newly discovered cultures. The early medieval monasteries regularly sent members to establish foundations in non-Christian areas of Europe and convert the population there. In the sixteenth century, both the mendicant orders and the newly founded apostolic orders evangelized people in Asia and the Americas. As recently as 1992, of the 5,441 U.S. Catholic missionaries ministering overseas, only 8 percent were lay missionaries, and only 3 percent were diocesan priests. The rest were either women religious (41 percent), religious priests (40 percent), or religious brothers (8 percent) (Siewert and Kenyon 1993:493). At home, religious orders like the Jesuits, Vincentians, and Redemptorists evangelized rural peasants, urban workers, and immigrants in both seventeenth-century Europe and the nineteenth-century Americas. Religious orders were also pioneers of health care throughout Europe from the time of the Dark Ages onwards. Nursing sisters were the first to begin hospitals in the United States, where one of their main concerns was to encourage deathbed repentance or conversion (Kauffman 1995:25, Wittberg 2006:30). Other members of religious orders created or popularized religious devotions such as the rosary, Forty Hours, parish missions, and novenas to the Sacred Heart or particular saints (Finke and Wittberg 2000:162).

This book argues that religious life is similarly necessary to the Catholic Church today. But it will necessarily exist in new and varied forms, which speak to the spiritual hungers of different societies, ethnic cultures, and generations. In the past several decades, national studies have been conducted to examine what has attracted the youngest and newest entrants to religious institutes. It is likely that young adults in each country, having been born into and come to adulthood within a culture that is profoundly different than that experienced by older religious, will have spiritual hungers and preferences for religious practice that are different from those of their elders. Religious institutes in each country will have to adjust to meet them. But while the generational studies have been done in each national setting, a cross-national meta-analysis of the studies has not yet been done. Societal and cultural changes have differently impacted different countries, and the kind of religious life that answers the spiritual hungers and preferences of young Catholics in one nation, one class, or one ethnic/cultural group may not appeal elsewhere.

The current book, therefore, begins by comparing studies that have been done of women who have entered religious institutes in Australia, Canada, France, Ireland, the United Kingdom, and the United States since the year 2000. The first of these studies was conducted in 2009 in the United States, with a follow-up study in 2019. The other national studies were conducted between 2009 and 2017. Some of the studies included quantitative surveys; others were based on transcriptions of interviews and focus groups. In addition, surveys and interviews were conducted with the major superiors of the institutes, and with the sisters who were engaged in vocation ministry and the formation of new entrants.

The first part of the book analyzes and compares the findings of these studies. Chapter 2 will explore the comparable quantitative data from the surveys of major superiors and new members, describing the number of new members in the institutes and their average age, their educational and family background, and what had attracted them to religious life and to their particular institute. Chapter 3 will rely on the interview transcripts and the answers to the open-ended questions in each country's study, comparing generational differences between the entrants who entered their institutes while in their mid-twenties or younger with those who entered when they were much older. This chapter will also investigate whether generational differences are the same or different in the particular countries. Since some of the national studies asked about obstacles to vocation discernment and entrance, or about current difficulties with the institutes' formation programs for new members, Chapter 4 will discuss and compare these findings. Chapter 5 will largely concentrate on the impact of cultural coherence or dissonance on the survival, flourishing, or decline of religious vocations in the United Kingdom and Ireland. The chapters in this part, therefore, are limited to findings on religious life as it exists today in the secularizing countries which trace their Christian roots to Western Europe.

The second part of the book will contain summaries of similar studies conducted in Mexico, India, and Kenya. In Chapter 6, Fr. Luis Fernando Falcó, MSpS, reports on why young women in Mexico are less likely than previous generations to consider religious life as a vocational option. In Chapter 7, Sr. Metti Amirthan, SCC, describes the findings of interviews conducted with one hundred sisters in India, while in Chapter 8 Sr. Bibiana Ngundo, LSOSF, reports on her study of new entrants to religious life in Kenya. Following the reports from research conducted in these three countries, two concluding chapters provide essays from the perspective of vocation promoters and formation personnel. In Chapter 9, Margaret Cartwright describes the situation of religious vocation in Ireland, where increasing secularization means that "For young people to celebrate their faith or even acknowledge it is seen as countercultural." In Chapter 10, Sr. Ellen Dauwer, SC, discusses the implications of the research for formation programs in the various countries. Finally, Chapter 11 concludes the book by discussing how the call of God to vowed religious life is felt universally, and how it is filtered through the specific cultural, economic, and demographic situation in each country.

In every time and place, religious life has been essential to the Church's survival and growth. The form which these institutes take, the practices and spiritualities which attract young (or not-so-young) people to join them, and the benefits and services they provide to the Church may vary. We hope that this comparative analysis and reflection will increase awareness of and appreciation for the many and varied roles religious institutes perform today.

We would also like to express our thanks and gratitude to Sister Mary Johnson, SND de N, who was the inspiration and the driving force behind this project. Even though she has not been able to contribute to writing the chapters, due to her election as Congregational Leader of the Sisters of Notre Dame de Namur in 2021, it was she who first recognized the potential in comparing the national studies and who recruited and convened us to accomplish the task. Sr. Mary was inspired by a conversation with Carol Schuck Scheiber, editor of *HORIZON*, the journal of the National Religious Vocation Conference, to consider a meta-analysis of these national studies to broaden our understanding of religious vocation on a more global scale. We are grateful to both of them and to the action of the Holy Spirit that has brought about this work.

2

Comparing Institutes of Women Religious and Their Newer Members

As described in the introduction, this book presents a meta-analysis of many recent studies of institutes of women religious and their newer members across several Western countries. Each of these studies investigates these institutes and their newer members to learn more about what is attracting contemporary women to religious life and what are some principal hindrances to consideration of such a vocation. A meta-analysis is simply a synthesis of the data from studies that are similar to one another in order to learn what factors are common among the studies and what factors stand out as distinctive. The aim of this meta-analysis is to provide a better understanding, sort of a "best guess" if you will, of what are the important "pull" and "push" factors that influence discernment of a vocation to religious life among contemporary women religious in economically advanced Western countries.

The first of the studies in this meta-analysis is a study of religious institutes and their newer members that was conducted in the United States in 2009 (Bendyna and Gautier 2009). The methodology and many of the questions from the two survey instruments used in this study (one for major superiors and the other for new members), were also used in a study conducted in 2015 in France (Gourant et al. 2023), another conducted in 2015 in Australia (Dixon et al. 2018), another conducted in 2017 in Canada (Kramarek and Gautier 2018), and a 2019 follow-up study conducted in the United States (Gautier and Do 2020). In addition, this meta-analysis includes another quantitative study conducted solely among major superiors in Australia in 2009 (Reid et al. 2010) and two qualitative studies conducted in the United Kingdom and in Ireland (Sexton and Simmonds 2015; Simmonds and Muñoz 2020) around the same time period (late 2000s). This chapter explores the comparable quantitative data from the surveys of major superiors and of new members, investigating first the insights from the major superiors' studies and then the insights from the studies of new members.

Institutes of Women Religious

A religious institute is a generic term for a unit of autonomous governance. This could be a religious order, congregation, monastery, province, region, or some other similar unit of women who profess canonical vows, which is governed by or accountable to a major superior (or one of similar title and corresponding authority). The purpose of the surveys of major superiors was primarily to learn about the membership and demographics of each institute and to study what each institute was doing in the area of vocations ministry. A secondary purpose of these surveys was to inform the major superiors of the larger study of newer members that was to be conducted and either to solicit the contact information for their newer members or to request that they distribute the survey to their newer members themselves, depending on the methodology used for each study. Some of the studies also conducted focus groups or interviews with selected major superiors, to provide more in-depth information about membership and vocations ministry. What follows here is a country-level comparison of the characteristics of these institutes of women religious.

Institute Size

As table 2.1 illustrates, there are many more institutes of women religious in the United States than there are in either Australia or in Canada, for historical and sociopolitical reasons that are not pertinent to this meta-analysis.[1] What is important to note here, though, is that at least half to two-thirds of all institutes of women religious within each country responded to each of the surveys. This is an excellent response rate, which allows for considerable confidence that the responses given accurately represent the responses of all women religious in those particular countries.

Table 2.1 Characteristics of Institutes of Women Religious Responding to the Surveys

	2009 USA	2009 AUS	2015 AUS	2017 CAN	2019 USA
Units of women religious responding	429	121	59	119	353
Approximate percentage responding among all units	50%	50%	64%	50%	67%
Median size of institute	56	29	N/A	21	43

Although the number of responding institutes varies considerably, the relative size of each institute is quite comparable. Canadian and Australian institutes tend to be somewhat smaller than U.S. institutes, but not dramatically so. In 2009, half of all responding U.S. institutes reported 56 or more members, compared to the responding Australian institutes, who reported 29 or more members. Half of all responding Canadian institutes had 21 or more members in 2017, about half as many as the 43 members reported by responding U.S. institutes in 2019. Note that the median[2] size of U.S. institutes declined between 2009 and 2019. This is an important point of reference because data from these studies and elsewhere

---

1. Institute-level data from the 2015 study conducted in France were not available to the authors for this project.
2. The median represents the midpoint of a distribution. In other words, if all responding U.S. institutes in 2019 were arranged according to membership, half of the institutes would have 43 or more members and half would have 43 or less members.

indicate that the total number of religious institutes, as well as the total number of women religious, has been declining in each of these countries and elsewhere in Europe since at least 1970 (*Annuarium Statisticum Ecclesiae* 2019). This fact, and the attendant questions about its causes and cure, have been the impetus for these and many other recent studies of Catholic religious institutes.

Numbers in Initial Formation

Comparing the numbers of full members (those in perpetual vows) to those in initial formation for religious life (i.e., candidates/postulants, novices, those in temporary vows) illustrates clearly that chief among the many reasons why religious institutes in these Western countries are decreasing in size and number is the fact that they have relatively few women currently in initial formation (see table 2.2). This is another fact of religious institutes in Europe, North America, and Canada that is evident in these surveys of major superiors and is also supported by *Annuarium Statisticum Ecclesiae* statistics, reported by the Vatican since 1970 (not shown here). This comparison is a bit misleading, though. Looking just at the ratio of perpetually professed members to those in initial formation in each country, it would appear that Australian institutes are in the best shape, with one in formation for every 12 perpetually professed, and that Canadian institutes are in dire straits, with one in formation for every 61 perpetually professed members. U.S. institutes appear to be somewhere in between, with one in formation for every 39 perpetually professed in 2009, and improving to one to 27 in 2019. Note that there are fewer full members *and* fewer in formation in U.S. institutes over this ten-year period: the real story here is that the large number of elderly members in U.S. institutes are dying off more rapidly than newer members are entering, which results in a slightly improved ratio. This is not a "good news" story for U.S. institutes, either.

Table 2.2 Characteristics of Members in Institutes of Women Religious Responding to the Surveys

	2009 USA	2009 AUS	2015 AUS	2017 CAN	2019 USA
Total members in perpetual vows	47,111	5,927	2,674	6,620	29,721
Total numbers in initial formation	1,206	N/A	218	108	1,085
Ratio of full members to those in initial formation	39:1	N/A	12:1	61:1	27:1
Median entrants in last 15 years	7	N/A	N/A	2	8
Retention rate for new members	50%	80%	63%	75%	69%

Most of the major superiors in these studies report that they have had no new entrants to the institute in the last fifteen years. Among those who do report having had at least one new entrant, half of the responding U.S. institutes report only seven (in 2009) or eight (in 2019) or less in the last fifteen years. For Canada, the responding institutes with at least one new entrant report only two or less in the last fifteen years. The retention rate for these new members (i.e., the proportion of those in initial formation who persist to perpetual vows in religious life) ranges from about half to 80 percent. This suggests that although the numbers entering these religious institutes in recent years are but a fraction of those who entered fifty years ago, they are apparently quite serious about their commitment as most of them persist through about eight years of formation to achieve perpetual profession in religious life.

Age and Nativity of Institute Members

Because most current members of religious institutes entered religious life more than fifty years ago, the median age of perpetually professed members in these Western institutes is now mid-to-late seventies. This is a consistent finding across each of the studies, which is also reflected in anecdotal data from other religious institutes in European countries. This reality means that nearly all of these religious institutes are struggling to fill institute leadership roles and facing other challenges of an increasingly aging membership.

14   God's Call Is Everywhere

Table 2.3 Age and Nativity of Members in Institutes of Women Religious

	2009 USA	2009 AUS	2015 AUS	2017 CAN	2019 USA
Median age of perpetually professed members	74	74	N/A	75	78
Percentage of members age 75 or older (70+ for USA)	69%	48%	47%	53%	83%
Percentage of members under age 45 (49 or younger for USA)	3%	4%	4%	1%	4%
Percentage of members who are native-born	N/A	75%	N/A	68%	N/A

The data in table 2.3 illustrate that about half of perpetually professed members (in Australia and Canada) to more than eight in ten (in the United States) are at retirement age or older. This means that these institutes, and their leaders, must focus an increasing share of their limited time and resources on caring for older members, which most often means less time and resources for ministry, evangelization, vocations, and other priorities. And looking at the percentage of members who are under age fifty, the ideal age for institute leadership and active ministry, these institutes have less than 5 percent of their members available to fill these important roles.

In a small way, some of the shortfall in members in these Western religious institutes is being compensated for by non-native members joining these institutes. In Australia, major superiors report that about a quarter of their perpetually professed members are from countries outside Australia, most often from predominantly Catholic countries in Asia and Africa. Canada, likewise, has about a third of members who come from outside Canada, most often from Asia, Africa, Latin America, or Europe. The two U.S. surveys of major superiors did not ask about the country of origin of members, but another national survey of the major superiors of U.S. institutes of women religious from 2015 reported that 8 percent of all active members of these institutes were born in another country (Johnson et al. 2019:30). There is historical precedent for this pattern of non-native religious being sent to mission territory in non-Catholic countries to provide for the education and social needs of immigrant Catholics and gradually being replaced by native vocations as the Catholic culture matures (see Wittberg 1994). In more recent decades, it is becoming more common for religious from countries where Catholicism is growing most rapidly in the global South to be sent to minister in the economically developed countries of Europe, North America, and Australia, where Catholic culture appears to be waning in the face of increasing secularism (see Mbonu 2016). This is similar to the pattern emerging in the religious institutes examined in this meta-analysis.

This section explored the institute characteristics and member demographics in the three countries of this meta-analysis that had available quantitative data from their institutes of women religious. The data show that, regardless of the number of institutes or their relative size, these institutes are largely comprised of an aging membership that is gradually being replaced by a much smaller, and more culturally diverse, younger membership. It is to this smaller group of newer members that we now turn our attention.

Newer Members of Institutes of Women Religious

The same studies that surveyed major superiors of institutes of women religious also undertook investigations of the newer members of these institutes, with the sole exception of the 2009 study of religious institutes in Australia. In addition to the data from the U.S. studies in 2009 and 2019, the 2017 Canadian study, and the 2015 Australian study, a questionnaire that was nearly identical to the ones used in those studies was translated into French and distributed to the newer members of religious institutes in France who were ages forty and below. Thus, this meta-analysis contains comparable quantitative data from five different studies, in four different countries at four similar points in time. We begin this section with the demographics of the newer members in each of these studies, then compare them on their attitudes about religious life and ministry.

Sample Size, Median Age, and Nativity

While the absolute numbers of respondents from each of these surveys varies widely, from just under 50 new member respondents in Australia to nearly 1,000 in the United States, this range is not due to lack of interest in responding to a survey among newer members but rather a representation of the very small numbers of newer members available to be surveyed (see table 2.4). This fact is borne out by an examination of the response rates: 991 respondents to the 2009 U.S. survey represented just 40 percent of all identified newer members. By comparison, Canada's 68 respondents in 2017 represented well over half of the approximately 125 identified newer members in that country. And the 987 respondents to the 2019 U.S. survey, while fewer in number than those responding in 2009, actually represent 7 in 10 of all identified newer members there, an increase of 30 percent in the response rate.

Table 2.4 Characteristics of Newer Members Responding to the Surveys

	2009 USA	2015 FRA	2015 AUS	2017 CAN	2019 USA
Women religious respondents in dataset	991	447	45	68	987
Approximate response rate among identified religious	40%	N/A	N/A	54%	70%
Median age	44	35–40	35–45	42	34
Percentage born outside survey country	18%	48%	44%	44%	21%

Response rates were not provided by researchers in the 2015 French or Australian studies, although they are likely to be comparable to the other studies.

These newer members in religious institutes are roughly similar in age across all five studies, with about half in their mid-forties or below. It is important to keep in mind that the study in France included only religious ages forty and below, so that sample does not include any newer religious who entered after age forty. Nevertheless, over half of the women religious newer members in the French sample are over age thirty-five, very similar to the other countries.

Another defining characteristic of these newer members is the relatively high number that were born outside the country in which they now serve. Close to half of the respondents in France, Australia, and Canada were born in another country. The figure in the United States is about one in five, but this is still a much higher proportion than the 8 percent of foreign-born, perpetually professed members reported by religious superiors in a 2014 survey of U.S.-based institutes of women religious (Johnson et al. 2019:30). The numbers of newer members who are from a country other than the one in which they now live and minister has been growing over time, in each of these countries. While this increasing cultural and ethnic diversity brings a multitude of blessings to these religious institutes, it comes with its own set of challenges as many of these newer members must navigate learning to live religious life in community in a culture that may be very different from the one they knew in childhood.

Family Characteristics

Nearly all of these newer members in the United States and in Canada were raised in Catholic families (see table 2.5). By comparison, the percent raised Catholic is just over half among the Australian newer members (and the question was not asked in France). Among those who were not raised Catholic, on average they became Catholic in their mid-twenties.

Table 2.5 Education and Religious Upbringing of Newer Members

	2009 USA	2015 FRA	2015 AUS	2017 CAN	2019 USA
Percentage raised Catholic	89%	N/A	52%	94%	91%
Mean age became Catholic (if not born Catholic)	26	N/A	25-30	27	25
Percentage ever home-schooled	4%	N/A	11%	0%	14%
Attended Catholic elementary school	56%	N/A	N/A	57%	46%
Attended Catholic high school	42%	N/A	N/A	57%	36%
Attended Catholic college	38%	N/A	N/A	32%	38%

Most of these newer members attended a Catholic school, at some level, while they were growing up. About half attended a Catholic elementary school, at least a third attended a Catholic high school, and about a third attended a Catholic college. The questions about Catholic schooling were not asked on the Australian survey or on the French survey. Catholic schools play a major role in education in Australia, however, and enroll about 20 percent of all school-aged children (https://ncec.catholic.edu.au/wp-content /uploads/2022/12/NCEC-2021-Annual-Report.pdf). Home schooling, an increasing trend in the United States, is still rare in other countries. While as many as 14 percent of newer members in the United States say they were home schooled, none of the Canadian newer members had been home schooled, and about one in ten in Australia had been home schooled. The question was not asked of newer members in France.

Experiences Before Entering Religious Life

These newer members of religious institutes had quite a bit of life experience before they entered religious life, unlike those of preceding generations who were likely to enter religious life right out of high school. On average, these newer members first considered religious life in their late teens or early twenties (see table 2.6). They entered their institutes about ten years later, on average, in their late twenties or mid-thirties.

Table 2.6 Experiences of Newer Members Before Entering Religious Life

	2009 USA	2015 FRA	2015 AUS	2017 CAN	2019 USA
Average age first considered religious life	20	19	15–19	22	18
Average age at entrance to religious institute	32	N/A	N/A	38	29
Percentage post–high school education before entering	85%	80%	80%	84%	89%
Percentage ever worked before entering	90%	45%	91%	99%	86%
If worked before entering, percentage full-time	82%	75%	71%	75%	73%
Volunteered in a parish or other setting	54%	30%	68%	57%	58%
Volunteered in a religious institute	9%	10%	23%	9%	10%
Attended a World Youth Day	13%	45%	30%	31%	22%
Percentage ever married	10%	0%	11%	13%	N/A

At least eight in ten had some postsecondary education before entering and many had careers. This education level is much greater than that for newer entrants in other parts of the world where higher education is less accessible. For example, in the essay from Africa later in this book, Sr. Bibiana Ngundo notes that just over half of the Kenyan newer entrants in 2017 had only a high school certificate or less when they entered religious life. Not quite half of the French newer members had work experience, compared to about nine in ten newer members in the United States and in Australia. Nearly all of the Canadian newer members had work experience, and three in four of them worked full-time before entering their institute, a similar proportion to those in the other countries.

Quite a few of them had volunteer experience in a parish or with other religious before they entered their institute. Two in three of the Australian newer members had volunteered in a parish or other setting before entering, quite similar to the newer members in Canada and the United States. Three in ten French newer members have volunteered in a parish or other setting. About one in ten had volunteered with a religious institute, and about one in four Australians had that experience.

Many of them had attended a World Youth Day before entering their institute, either as a participant or as a young adult chaperone. The proportion ranges from about one in ten newer members in the United States to nearly half of French newer members.

Some of them had been married before they entered religious life. None of the French newer members had been married, but the French sample excluded anyone who was over age forty. In the other countries, about one in ten had been married before they entered.

Attraction to Religious Life and to a Particular Religious Institute

These newer women religious were asked about the ways they felt called to religious life and their answers were strikingly similar. Nearly all agreed strongly that they were responding to a call from God (see figure 2.1). Nearly as many (76 to 83 percent) said they were "very much" attracted by their desire for prayer and spiritual growth. Six in ten were "very much" attracted by their desire to be part of a community. We will see a similar pattern in the responses from newer members in Kenya in the essay from Africa later in this book.

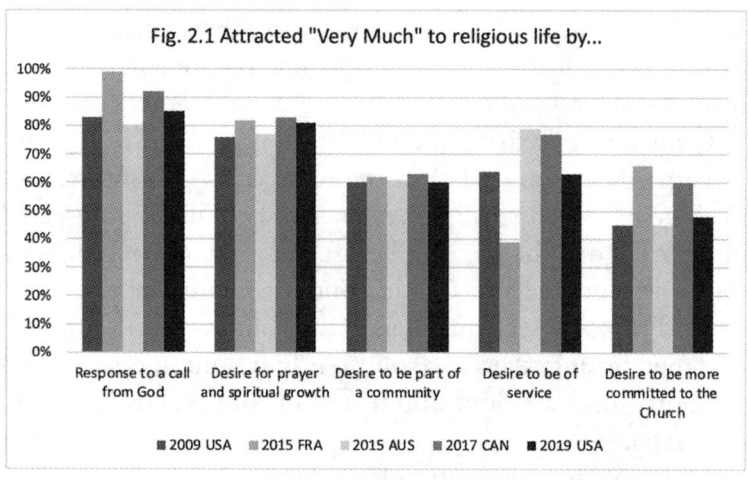

A desire to be of service "very much" attracted two-thirds to three-quarters of newer members from the United States, Australia, and Canada, but French respondents were less likely to be as attracted by a desire to be of service. On the other hand, two-thirds of the French newer members and three-fifths of the Canadian newer members were "very much" attracted by their desire to be more committed to the Church, compared to about half of the newer members in the other countries.

In contrast, the newer members differ quite a bit, by country, in the things that attracted them "very much" to their particular religious institute (see figure 2.2). Four of the defining aspects of religious life—the spirituality, the mission, the prayer life, and the community life—were aspects that most members across all countries said had attracted them to their particular religious institute.

The spirituality of the institute was the aspect that the greatest proportion of newer members said had "very much" attracted them to their institute in all countries except Australia, with about three-quarters to nine in ten reporting that they were "very much" attracted by this, compared to 68 percent in Australia. The aspect of their religious institute that the greatest proportion of Australians said "very much" attracted them was its mission, mentioned by more than three in four. Newer members in France and Canada were similarly attracted to their institute by its mission (80 and 83 percent, respectively), but this was of less importance to respondents in the two U.S. surveys (about six in ten said that the mission of the institute "very much" attracted them).

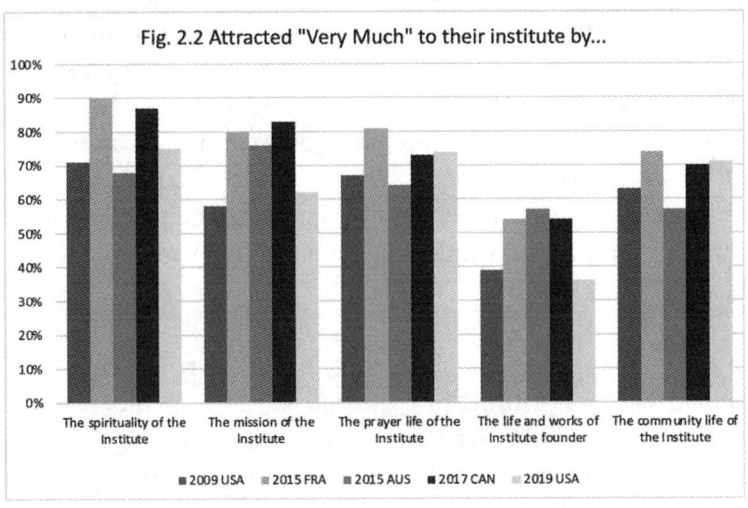

Likewise, the prayer life of their institute was similarly important across all five surveys, with about two in three to eight in ten finding it "very much" attracted them. The community life of the institute was similarly attractive, with about two in three to three in four finding it "very much" attracted them to their institute.

In contrast, aspects of their religious institute related to its charism, such as the life and works of its founder, appear to be less important to newer members in the United States than to those in France, Australia, and Canada. Just over a third of U.S. newer members said they were "very much" attracted to their institute by the life and works of its founder, compared to well over half of the newer members in France, Australia, and Canada. It could be that the particular charism of the institute, as expressed in the life and works of its founder, plays a lesser role in attracting new members to religious life in the U.S. because the much larger number of religious institutes there allows for many different expressions of the charism of a particular founder. For example, there are more than twenty institutes of Dominican sisters in the U.S., all attributing their founding to St. Dominic. Some of these institutes are composed of apostolic congregations of religious sisters and others are cloistered communities of contemplative nuns. Among the apostolic Dominican congregations, some institutions primarily taught in schools while others ministered to the sick. There is much less variation in the expression of charism among the smaller number of institutes located in France, Australia, and Canada.

Adding some evidence to this speculation, newer members in the U.S. appear to be more strongly attracted to their particular religious institute by the example of the members of the institutes that they have come to know and by the welcome and encouragement they have received from its members. These personalities are more appealing to newer members than the life and works of the institute founder (see figure 2.3).

This personal example is important across all countries, but less so in Australia, where just about half said that the example of its members attracted them "very much" to their institute. About two-thirds of the newer members in the other countries said this. And the welcome and encouragement by members, which six in ten newer members in the U.S. said "very much" attracted them to their institute, was by far the least important aspect attracting newer members in France and Australia.

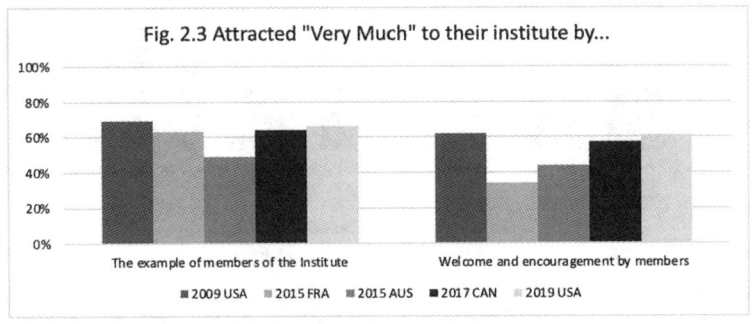

Fig. 2.3 Attracted "Very Much" to their institute by...
■ 2009 USA ■ 2015 FRA ■ 2015 AUS ■ 2017 CAN ■ 2019 USA

Learning About and Discerning Their Place in Religious Life

The most common way that newer members first became acquainted with the sisters with whom they live and work was through an institute where these members served, such as a school, hospital, or other sponsored ministry of the religious institute (see figure 2.4). Between a fifth and a third on each survey indicated this response. Respondents in Canada, however, were more likely to say that they first became acquainted with their institute through the recommendation of a friend or advisor (38 percent) than to say that they first became acquainted through an institute where members served (21 percent). Less commonly, introductions came through working with a member of the institute, an event sponsored by the institute, or having a relative or a friend who was a member of the institute. Few said they first became acquainted with their institute through a media story or some other print or online promotional material.

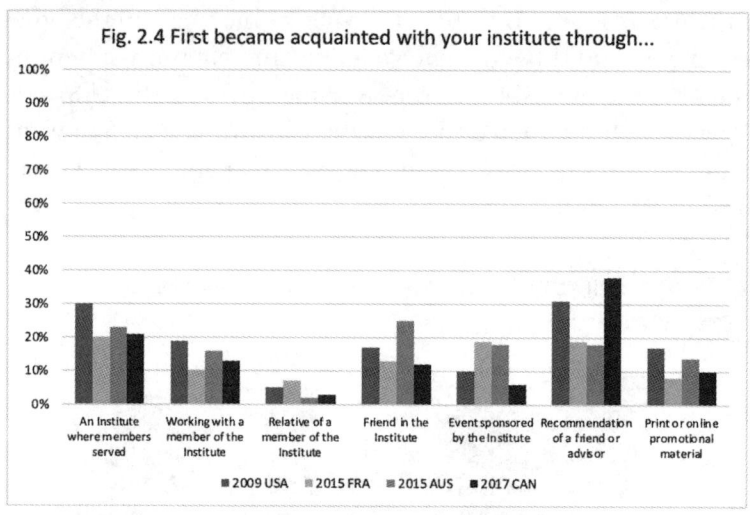

Reinforcing the importance of personal contact in influencing discernment to a particular institute, more than half of newer members said that they took part in a "Come and See" experience or a live-in experience with their institute before entering formally. While few newer members in France mentioned a "Come and See" experience (known as "Open Doors" in that country), most likely because the experience is relatively new there, almost two in three French newer members took part in a live-in experience with their institute (see figure 2.5).

Spiritual direction is also an important part of discernment, and between 60 and 70 percent of newer members took part in spiritual direction before entering their institute (the question was not asked on the 2019 U.S. survey). Around a third of newer members also took part in regular meetings with a vocation director, with other members of their institute, and made regular visits to their communities before entering (these questions were not asked on the 2019 U.S. survey).

Although they took part in a variety of experiences during their discernment, which of these experiences proved valuable to them for discerning a vocation to religious life? Not all experiences were equally valuable (see figure 2.6). Only about a quarter or less found websites (such as diocesan or general Catholic websites, vocation discernment websites, or religious institute websites) even somewhat helpful. Close to half or more of respondents in Australia, Canada, and the U.S. in 2019, however, found religious institute websites to be at least somewhat helpful to their discernment (not shown in figure). Newspaper or magazine articles, CDs, DVDs, and diocesan vocation programs were not helpful either.

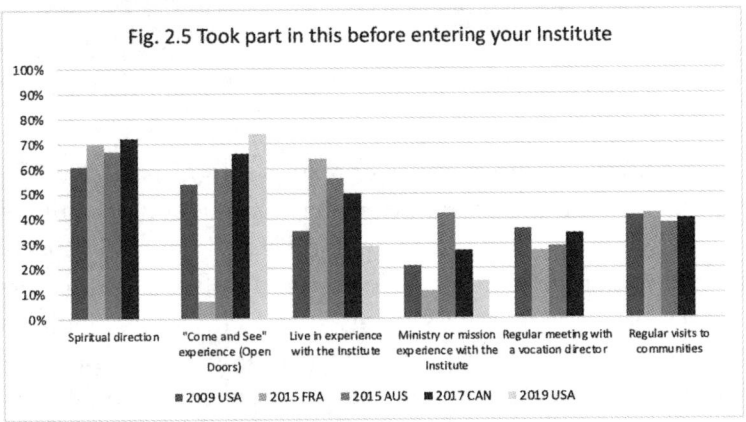

Fig. 2.5 Took part in this before entering your Institute

What newer members did find helpful was spiritual direction, discernment retreats, meeting with a member of the institute, visits to communities, and "Come and See" or live-in experiences—all those personal interactions that first attracted them to their institute. Meeting with a vocation director was at least somewhat helpful for seven in ten 2009 U.S. and Canadian newer members but less so for French or Australian newer members. Four in ten French respondents found meeting with a discernment group to be helpful, compared to a third or less of newer members of the other countries (not shown in the figure).

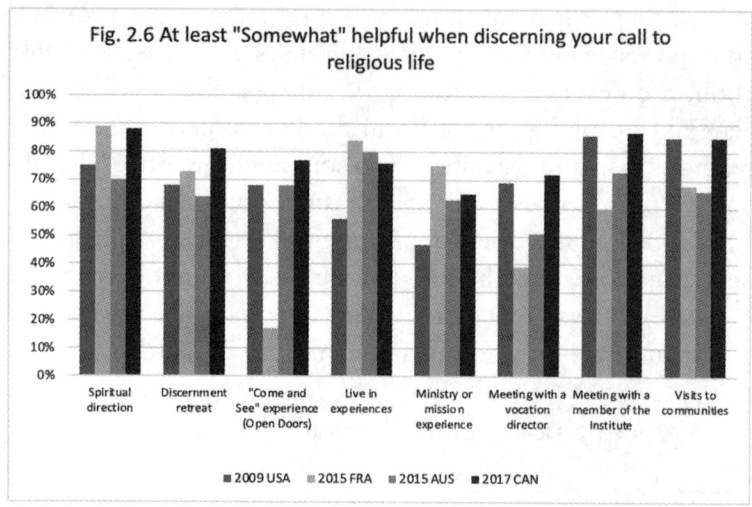

Fig. 2.6 At least "Somewhat" helpful when discerning your call to religious life

The final decision about entering religious life, while unique to each individual, does have some commonalities across countries. Beyond the personal and cultural aspects of each religious institute, which are manifested in the personalities of the members themselves, many other qualities factor into the final decision. For example, the single most important influencer among Canadian newer members is the charism of the institute founder, which was also very important among French and 2019 U.S. respondents (see figure 2.7). Although the question was not asked of Australian or 2009 U.S. respondents, we know from the qualitative data in these studies that the charism of the institute founder influenced these respondents very much as well.

Several other qualities of the institute, such as its prayer life, its community life, and the lifestyle of its members very much influenced half to two-thirds of newer members in each of these studies. The types of ministries of the institute were also very influential to the decision of at least a third, and more than half of French and Canadian respondents said this very much influenced their decision to enter their institute.

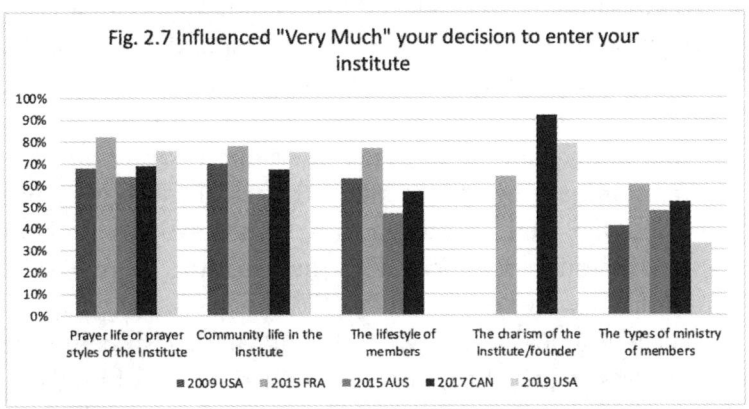

Fig. 2.7 Influenced "Very Much" your decision to enter your institute

Yet some aspects of the institute, which many might consider very important in a life-changing decision about which institute to enter—things such as the ages of its members, the size of the institute, its geographic location, and its internationality—were much less influential in the decision of these newer members. A fifth or less of any group said any of these factors very much influenced their decision to enter their institute (not shown in the figure).

Several other patterns emerge in comparing responses across countries:

- The French respondents were the most attracted to their institute by its spirituality and its prayer life (figures 2.2 and 2.7). They were the least likely to say they were attracted to religious life by a desire to be of service (figure 2.1) or to have taken part in a ministry or mission experience (figure 2.5). But those who did take part in such experiences found them very helpful in their discernment, more so than the newer members in any other country (figure 2.6).

- The Australian respondents were the least attracted of all the countries' respondents by their institute's community life, although over half did list community as an attraction (figures 2.2, 2.7). Australian respondents were the most likely to cite a desire to be of service as something that had attracted them "very much" to religious life (figure 2.1), and among the most likely to say that the mission of the institute had attracted them to it (figure 2.2). They were also the most likely to have had ministry or mission experiences with their institute (figure 2.5). But they were somewhat less likely to rank these experiences as at least "somewhat helpful" in their discernment process (figure 2.6), or to say that the type of ministry their institute engaged in was what influenced them to enter it (figure 2.7).

- Canadian respondents, like the Australians, were very much attracted to religious life by a desire to be of service (figure 2.1) and by the mission of their institute (figure 2.2). About one in four respondents took part in a ministry or mission experience (figure 2.5), which most found at least "somewhat helpful" in discerning their call to religious life and to their institute (figure 2.6). This was the highest proportion after the Australians. Like the French, however, the Canadian respondents were also attracted by the spirituality and the prayer life of their institute (figure 2.2), although they were less likely than the French to say that this "very much" influenced their desire to enter (figure 2.7)

- The U.S. respondents fell midway between the French and the Australians in citing a desire to be of service as an attraction to religious life (figure 2.1), but they were the least likely in both years to say they were attracted by their institute's mission (figure 2.2) or by its ministry (figure 2.7). They were less likely than the French and Canadians to say they were "very much" attracted to their institute by its spirituality or prayer life in the 2009 survey (figures

2.2 and 2.7). However, their attraction to both these dimensions increased between 2009 and 2019, so that they surpassed the Canadian respondents in the latter year.

Encouragement in Religious Life, Before and after Entering

Most people seek out others for advice and encouragement when they are discerning a religious vocation. When asked about who encouraged them when they were considering entering a religious institute, newer members from each group were most likely to say that they received "very much" encouragement from their spiritual advisor and from members of the religious institute they were considering (see figure 2.8). At least half to three quarters mentioned receiving "very much" encouragement from these two sources. About half to two-thirds received as much encouragement from their vocation director or vocation team, except in the case of French newer members.

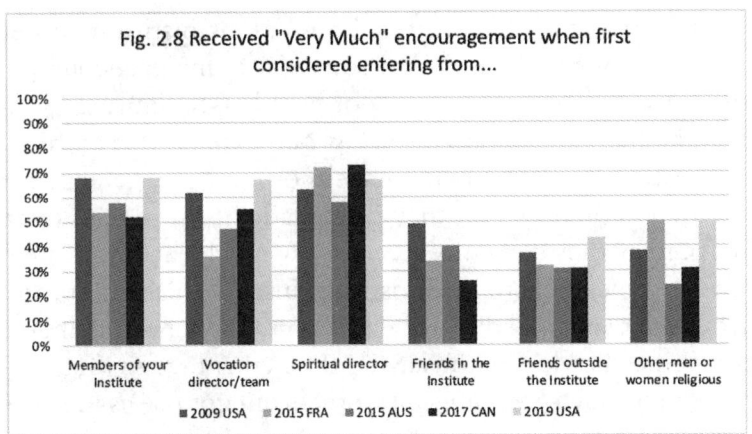

Fig. 2.8 Received "Very Much" encouragement when first considered entering from...

Half of newer members in France and in the U.S. in 2019 received "very much" encouragement from other men or women religious, although fewer participants from the other countries agreed as much. Friends, both inside and outside the institute, were less likely to have been as encouraging to these newer members when they were entering. Around a third, or fewer, newer members mentioned diocesan priests, people in their parish, people in their school or workplace, or family members as being very encouraging to them when they first considered entering (not shown in the figure).

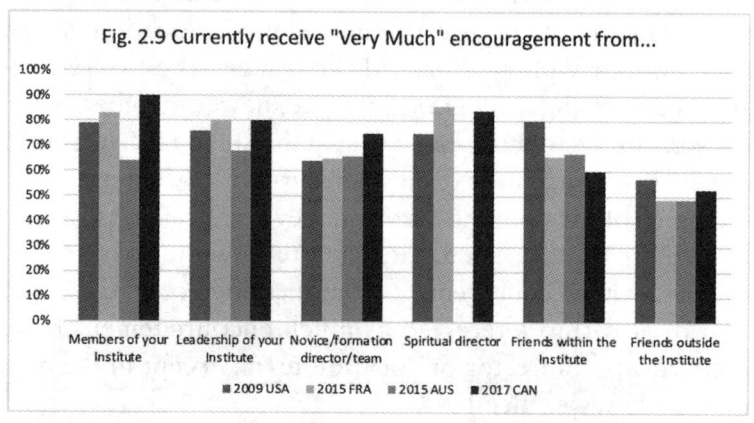

Fig. 2.9 Currently receive "Very Much" encouragement from...

Now that they have entered a religious institute, newer members mostly say that they receive very much encouragement from these same groups of people (see figure 2.9). In fact, higher percentages in each group express this opinion, suggesting that they experience more encouragement for their decision now that they have made it. More than three in four say they currently receive very much encouragement from the members of their institute, institute leadership, and from their spiritual director. The Australian newer members are somewhat less enthusiastic; the percentage saying they were very much encouraged by others did not rise as much as the responses of newer entrants in other countries did. Still, about two in three Australian respondents say they currently receive very much encouragement from their institute, its leadership, and their spiritual director. About two-thirds to three-fourths receive very much encouragement from their novice director, across all groups. U.S. respondents are particularly likely to say they currently receive very much encouragement from friends, both within and outside their institute.

Even the other groups, which newer members indicated were not particularly encouraging of them when they were discerning, are now giving them very much encouragement in their vocation (see figure 2.10). In particular, half to two-thirds of newer members say they currently receive very much encouragement from parents, siblings, people with whom they minister, and people to whom they minister. Australian and French newer members are less likely than the other groups to say they currently receive very much encouragement from diocesan priests, people in their parish, people in their school or workplace, or from other family members.

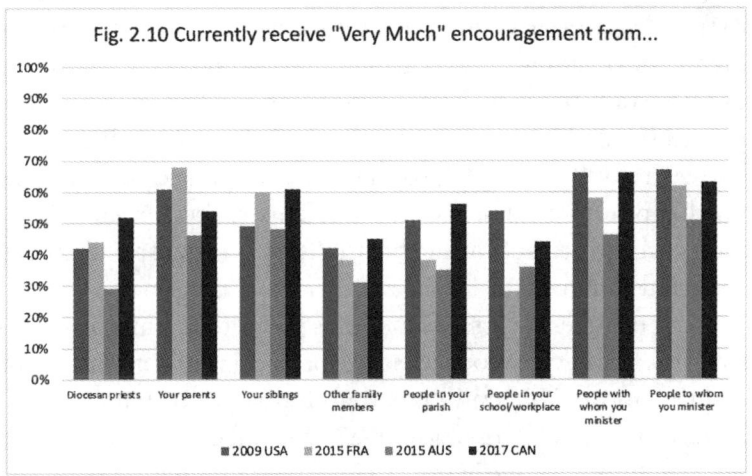

Fig. 2.10 Currently receive "Very Much" encouragement from...

Current Religious Environment

Now that they are becoming established in their religious vocation, what are the aspects of religious life that these newer members find particularly important? Nearly all, across all groups, agree that praying together, living together, sharing meals, and socializing or sharing leisure time together are very important to them, a reflection of how important their institute's community life had been in attracting them to enter (cf. figures 2.2 and 2.7). Working together is also very important to between two-thirds and three-fourths of newer members, except in the case of Australia, where just under half say that working with other members is very important to them. With the small number of religious who are spread very thin across their ministry sites, working together is an unrealistic expectation for most Australian sisters.

The type of prayer that is very important to newer members across all the countries is daily Eucharist, followed closely by Liturgy of the Hours (see figure 2.11). Australian newer members are a bit of an exception to this pattern, as they are more likely to say that faith sharing is very important to them than to say that Liturgy of the Hours is very important. Eight in ten French and U.S. newer members say that Eucharistic Adoration is very important to them, and French newer members are equally likely to say that common meditation is as important to them. The value which the U.S. respondents placed on daily Mass and Eucharistic Adoration increased between 2009 and 2019, so that the 2019 respondents' data on this point surpassed Canada's. This reflects a similar increase in the attraction of spirituality to U.S. respondents as reported in figures 2.1 and 2.2.

Most members across all countries prefer to live in a medium-sized community of four to seven or in a large community of eight or more. Very few (less than a quarter of participants, across all countries) prefer to live in a small community of two or three, and only one in ten or fewer prefer to live alone. As for their preferred living setting, more than half of newer members across all countries prefer "very much" to live in community with other members of their institute. A third to about half (in the case of France) "very much" prefer to live in community with members of other units of their institute. Living with members of other institutes or living with lay associates is the preferred living setting for only about a tenth or slightly more of newer members.

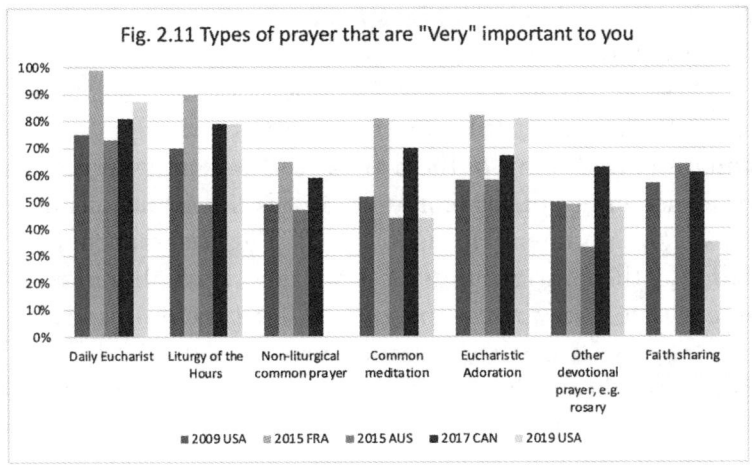

Fig. 2.11 Types of prayer that are "Very" important to you

As for the composition of their living setting, more than half of newer members across all countries very much prefer living with members of different ages, which is the reality in nearly all religious communities today (see figure 2.12). With the exception of 2019 U.S. newer members, more than half of the others very much prefer living with members of different cultures, and around half very much prefer living with members in different ministries.

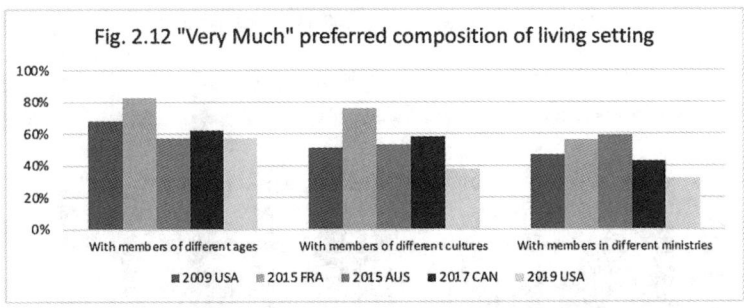

Fig. 2.12 "Very Much" preferred composition of living setting

These three characteristics—living with members of different ages, from different cultures, and in different ministries—increasingly define religious life today in all of these countries. It is encouraging to see that these newer members are embracing this diversity in religious life.

Evaluation of Their Religious Institute by Newer Members

These newer members will be the ones shaping the future of religious institutes in their countries in the years to come—indeed, some of them are already assuming positions of leadership in their communities. It is important to know how they evaluate their institutes: Do they feel that they are fulfilling their various missions? What is the quality of community life? Are there opportunities for growth in spiritual life? How well are their institutes providing for the needs of newer members? These and other similar questions were also asked of these newer members.

A majority of newer members across all countries agree that their institute is "excellent" in its life of fidelity to the Church and its teachings (see figure 2.13). More than half (except for France) agree that their institute is "excellent" at instilling a sense of identity as institute members. Canadians are more likely than newer members in other countries to say that their institute excels in its response to the needs of our time, although at least two-thirds of newer members in other countries except for France agree as strongly.

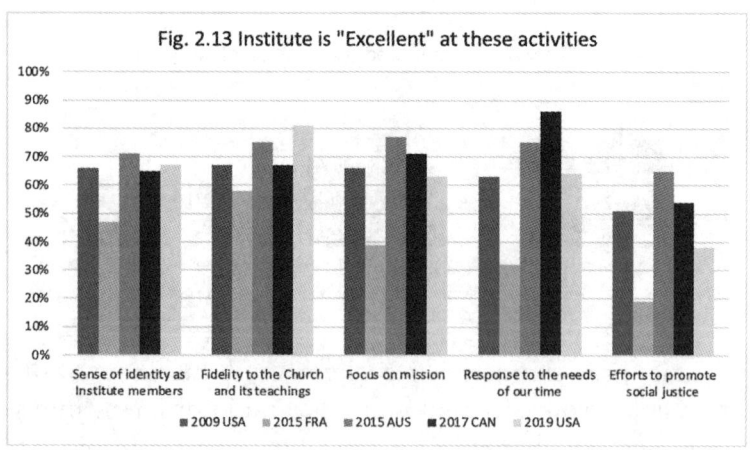

Indeed, French newer members judge their institutes more harshly than do other countries on all these measures. While two-thirds to three-fourths of newer members in the U.S., Canada, and Australia say their institute is "excellent" in its focus on mission, just four in ten French newer members say the same. Finally, while about two-thirds of 2009 U.S. and Australian and just over half of Canadian newer members say that their institute is "excellent" in its efforts to promote social justice, that proportion drops to two in five for U.S. (in 2019) and one in five for French newer members. This suggests that promoting social justice may be an increasing source of concern and initiative among these newer members.

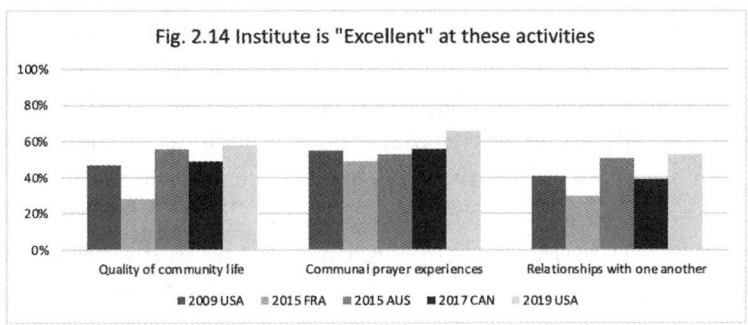

Fig. 2.14 Institute is "Excellent" at these activities

The more essential aspects of religious life, intrinsic to its very definition and certainly central to these newer members since these were the very aspects that drew them to religious life in the first place—community life, prayer life, and living in relationship to others with shared values—are all aspects that could be improved upon, according to a plurality of these newer members (see figure 2.14). About half to two-thirds of newer members in each country say that their institute is "excellent" in its communal prayer experiences. Similarly, around half of newer members in all countries but France agree that their institute is "excellent" in the quality of its community life. But only about half of Australian and U.S. (in 2019) newer members, and lesser percentages in the other countries, agree that their institute is "excellent" in its relationships with one another. This could be an area for improvement, according to many of these newer members.

Some other aspects of religious life, intrinsic to personal and spiritual growth, are evaluated more highly by these newer members (see figure 2.15). For example, seven in ten to eight in ten report that their institute is "excellent" in its opportunities for spiritual growth (although half as many French respondents rate their institute as highly on this aspect). And half to three-quarters say their institute excels in its faithfulness to prayer and spiritual growth. Likewise, two in three or more in each country (but three in ten among French newer members) evaluate their institute as "excellent" in its sense of identity as religious and in its opportunities for personal growth. Most newer members in all countries but France feel that their institute is doing an excellent job in these aspects of religious life. In fairness, a plurality of French newer members (four in ten or more) rated their institute as at least "good" on each of these aspects, which suggests that they are not, in fact, dissatisfied with their religious institute in these aspects but perhaps see more opportunity for improvement.

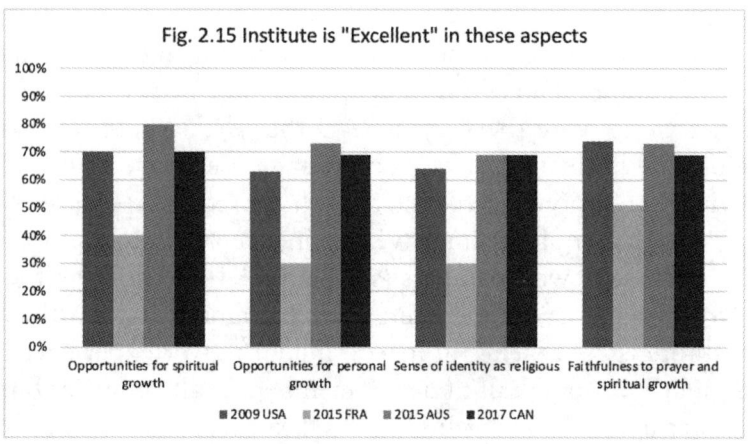

Finally, how do these newer members evaluate their institutes on various aspects related to attracting new members, forming them for mission, and providing for their initial and ongoing formation? While a majority evaluate their institute as "excellent" in most of these aspects, two in particular stand out as areas for improvement.

Efforts to promote vocations is one area that institutes could improve, according to these newer members (see figure 2.16). While more than half of U.S. respondents in 2019 say their institute is "excellent" in this aspect, less than half in each of the other countries agree as strongly with this evaluation. France and Australia stand out in their low evaluation of institute efforts to promote vocations. This is somewhat unusual for the Australians, approximately half of whom report that they themselves had received "very much" encouragement from members of their institution and from their institute's vocation director/team when they first considered entering (see figure 2.8).

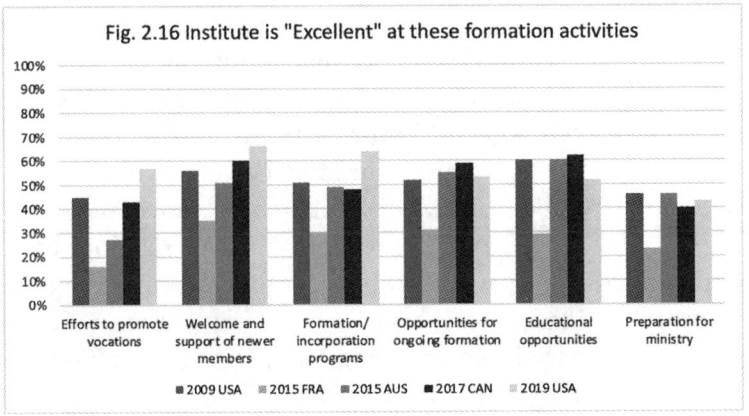

Fig. 2.16 Institute is "Excellent" at these formation activities

Likewise, less than half of newer members in any of the countries evaluate their institute as excellent in the way it prepares members for ministry. This is an aspect of the institute that many judge as opportune for improvement. This should come as no surprise, as these newer members are often the very ones chosen to step in and take on ministries for which they were not prepared as older sisters have to give up the ministries they have done for so many years.

At the same time, half to two-thirds of these newer members say their institute does an excellent job in welcoming and supporting newer members. About the same proportion evaluate their institute as highly on its formation and incorporation programs, its opportunities for ongoing formation, and on its educational opportunities. Again, French newer members are much less likely than those in the other countries to rate their institute as "excellent" on each of these aspects, but a plurality (40 percent or more) evaluate their institute as at least "good" on each aspect. It could be that this is more of a cultural attribute than a harsher evaluation among the French newer members, especially since it shows up so consistently across all these evaluative questions.

Conclusion

Across these countries, we see many more similarities than differences in religious institutes and the newer members who are entering religious life today. The institutes face similar challenges of aging membership, few newer members entering, and increasing cultural diversity among newer members. They also encounter the very real promise that religious life is not going away—newer members continue to enter religious institutes and transform them by their very presence. This is joyful news indeed, even for religious institutes that have not had a new member enter in decades.

The newer members in these countries, likewise, appear to have more similarities than differences. They are mostly in their thirties and forties, much younger than most of the other sisters in their institute. Many of them were born in another country than the one where they now live and minister, and they bring a cultural and ethnic diversity to their institutes that is experienced as both a blessing and a challenge. They are well-educated and bring a wide variety of life skills and experience with them into religious life. This life experience, however, can also prove to be a challenge for some as they struggle to find their place in community life.

With some variation across countries, the newer members were attracted to religious life by similar desires for authentic community life, for communal prayer experiences, and a deep desire for meaningful ministry. They were drawn to their particular institute usually through personal interactions with its members and were encouraged by the welcome they received from members. Though they entered religious life via a variety of pathways, each has found meaning and fulfillment in the community life, the prayer life, and the mission of the institute they have chosen. They prefer living in community to living alone, even though life in a community of varying ages, ethnicities, and cultures can be challenging. They rate their institute highly in the ways that it expresses religious values and lives out religious life, but at the same time they recognize that there is room for improvement in their religious institute—indeed, a place where they can make a meaningful contribution to religious life.

This brief panorama of the demographics, pathways, attitudes, and preferences of newer members in religious life barely scratches the surface of what being a religious means to these women religious today. The next chapter digs into the qualitative data from these countries to learn more from their experiences and to hear about religious life in their own voices.

3

Generational Differences among Newer Entrants to Religious Life

To a large extent, human beings are shaped by the social locations in which they pass their childhood and adolescence, and which they confront—more or less reflectively—as they enter adulthood. Whether a child was born and raised in China or Brazil, in a wealthy enclave or in an impoverished slum, as a member of the dominant racial majority or of an oppressed minority, as male or female, in times of war and economic depression or in times of peace and prosperity, lead to the development of "broad, deep mental structures— world views, basic values, mindsets and characteristic ways of thinking" that children absorb without questioning them (Esler 1984:106; Dean 2010:45–49).

In his seminal essay on generational worldviews, Karl Mannheim postulated that only in late adolescence do young adults become cognitively mature enough to evaluate the mental structures they were exposed to in their childhood. They continue to accept the aspects that are consistent with their current experience of the world, but they question and reject the aspects that are not. This moment of "fresh encounter" can result in a particular, generation-specific outlook that distinguishes its possessors from persons who were formed in earlier or later periods, and it tends to resist change thereafter (Mannheim 1952 [1928]:298). Attitudes toward religious adherence, belief, and practice are part of these generationally and culturally specific worldviews. The stance which persons adopt toward religion in early adulthood will shape their involvement in churches and denominations for years to come (Wittberg 2021). It may also, therefore, influence whether and when Catholics choose to enter vowed religious life, and the kind of religious institute that attracts them.

This chapter will focus on the spiritual hungers and religious worldviews that distinguish Catholic women religious who grew up at different times and in different countries, and explore how these attitudes have influenced those who have joined vowed religious life in the first two decades of the twenty-first century. It will compare the different generations of the women entering religious institutes today: those who are currently entering when they are in their late fifties or older, those who are entering while in their forties and early fifties, those who are entering while in their thirties, and those who are in their twenties or younger. To the extent that they absorbed different religious worldviews and attitudes in their respective childhoods, do the older women currently entering religious institutes seek different models of religious life than the younger women do?

Since generational cohort is not the only social location that influences one's religious worldview and desires, we will also compare the views of the different generations of newly entered sisters in the United States, Canada, Australia, the United Kingdom, Ireland, and France. Where possible, we will look especially at the intersection of these two dimensions: do the generational fault lines affecting entrants to religious institutes in one country also exist for religious institutes of other countries, or are they different?

Attraction to Religious Life

Chapter 2 described the various studies upon which this book is based. Among the data gathered by these studies were the familial and religious backgrounds of women entering religious life in France, Australia, Canada, and the United States, and what had attracted them to religious life and to their particular religious institute. But the generational cohort to which the women belonged also influenced their vocational choices. For Catholics in the United States, possibly the most important influence on their conception of what being Catholic means, and of where their Catholic religious identity fits into their overall worldview and basic values, is whether they passed their formative years before, during, or after the Second Vatican Council's changes took effect. U.S. Catholics whose childhood socialization into their religion took place prior to the end of the Council, and who first experienced the Council's many changes in their adolescence and young adulthood, have different attitudes and expectations than later generations which did not experience pre–Vatican II Catholicism (D'Antonio et al. 2013). Studies in the United States have differentiated between this "Vatican II Generation" (born prior to 1961) and later age cohorts: the "post–Vatican II Generation" (born 1961–1980) whose childhood socialization as Catholics occurred during the initial time of upheaval after the Council, and the "Millennial Generation" (born 1981–1995) whose parents also had not been socialized in the pre–Vatican II Church (D'Antonio et al. 2013). It remains to be seen if young people born after 1995 (sometimes labeled "Generation Z") will have been sufficiently influenced by additional occurrences such as the environmental movement or the numerous Church sex scandals to comprise still another distinct generation of U.S. Catholics. It also remains to be seen whether the generational categories developed by researchers for U.S. Catholicism can be applied to other countries. In the United Kingdom, for example, Bullivant (2019:60) found that the sharpest decline in Catholic identification and adherence occurred between those born before and after 1945, with no pronounced difference between age cohorts thereafter. The decline in the number of young Catholics entering religious life also began earlier—before Vatican II—in Europe and the United Kingdom than it did in the United States. The analysis in the subsequent pages will compare Vatican II, post–Vatican II, and Millennial women—and, to a limited extent, Generation Z women—who have entered religious institutes in the past ten or fifteen years, to see whether there are similarities or differences across generation and across country.

Methodology

Overarching worldviews, values, and attitudes—toward religion or anything else—are too complex and multifaceted to be fully reflected in survey questions with a limited set of fixed responses (agree/disagree, never/sometimes/often, etc.). Fortunately, many of the national surveys analyzed here also included several open-ended questions, to which the sisters could write their own responses. Responses to open-ended survey questions were available for the United States, Canada, and Australia. The researchers in the United Kingdom and Ireland collected, recorded, and transcribed interview data, supplemented by a smaller number of open-ended survey responses. The French study includes transcripts of thirteen focus groups of young religious and formation personnel as they discuss their call to consecrated life.

For this chapter, the open-ended answers in the U.S. and Canadian surveys were compiled separately and grouped by the age of the responding sister. The answers were then read several times and the different themes in them were listed. A count was made of the number of times a particular theme was mentioned, and the percentage of the total respondents in each age cohort who mentioned that theme was calculated. Since Millennial sisters comprised by far the largest number of respondents in the 2019 U.S. survey, this age cohort was divided in half, to see if older Millennials differed from the younger members of their cohort. There were also enough Generation Z respondents (under age 24 in 2019) in the U.S. survey for this age cohort to be analyzed separately as well. This was not the case in the Canadian and Australian surveys. In the following two sections of this chapter, the figures given in the various tables are expressed as percentages of the varying number of respondents in each age category. In reading these figures, it should be noted that the percentage reported (e.g., 20 percent) does not mean that a given hope or concern was felt by only 20 percent of the respondents, but merely that 20 percent thought to mention it in their answer. In responses to open-ended questions, it is actually unusual, and worthy of notice, for a given topic to be spontaneously raised by as many as 20 percent of the respondents.

Findings by Country

The United States

The 2019 U.S. study contained two open-ended questions[1] that shed light on the differing mindsets which the sisters who have recently entered their institute bring to religious life:

- "Looking ahead ten years, what are your hopes for the future in your religious institute?"
- "What most concerns you about your future in religious life?"

---

1. A third open-ended question, "What are the greatest obstacles in vocation discernment for discerners and vocation directors?" is not included in this chapter's analysis. It will be discussed in chapter 4.

In 2019, recently-entered sisters born before 1961 would have been aged 59 or older. Those born between 1961 and 1980 would have ranged between 39 and 58 in age, while the Millennial Generation would have been between 24 and 38 years old. Generation Z respondents would have been younger than 24. While several themes in the sisters' answers were similar across all of these age cohorts, other themes showed pronounced differences across the generations.

By far the largest generational differences occur in the answers which mention the sisters' hopes and concerns about spiritual growth or fervor—primarily of the individual respondent, but also of her institute. As table 3.1 shows, the youngest (Generation Z) respondents are more likely to mention their own and their institute's growth in holiness or prayerfulness as their primary hope for the future, and by far the most likely to list "Loss of my fervor" as their greatest concern about their future in religious life. Concern over the loss of their institute's fervor increases sharply between the Vatican II and post–Vatican II generations, and then declines somewhat among the younger age cohorts. Even so, the youngest respondents are twice as likely as the Vatican II generation respondents to list this concern.

Table 3.1 Hopes and *Concerns* about the Future, by Generation

Hope/Concern	Vatican II (Age 59+) N=54 N=49 %	Post-Vatican II (Age 39–58) N=235 N=216 %	Millennials I (Age 31–38) N=277 N=259 %	Millennials II (Age 24–30) N=221 N=220 %	Gen Z (Age <24) N=42 N=39 %
Loss of my fervor	*10.2*	*18.5*	*32.8*	*40.0*	*64.1*
My growth in holiness	3.7	6.8	10.5	15.8	16.7
Loss of institute's fervor	*2.0*	*9.3*	*5.4*	*5.5*	*5.1*
Institute's growth in holiness	9.3	14.9	20.2	18.6	21.4

Samples of the respondents' concerns over future loss of fervor, both for themselves and for their institutes, include:

Worldliness threatens to choke us at all times. It is present within and around us. Technology and the media present

a dangerous threat that must be allowed into our cloisters up to a certain point, but it can shake our fidelity in very subtle ways. It presents a constant concern to those of us who have promised God to persevere until death. Even after perpetual vows, too many possibilities are offered to us. (Age 32)

What concerns me most is something bad happening to my community, such as falling away from our charism, purpose, and mission, or the spirit of activism getting in (as we are contemplatives) and not being all that God has called us to be. I also fear declining in members and not receiving new members. All of these would certainly be a threat to my own future in religious life. (Age 29)

The changes I see in other communities. I want to preserve what we have by living it faithfully. (Age 37)

The respondents' hopes for future growth in holiness/prayerfulness—both of the individual sister and of the institute—include:

I hope to have fallen more deeply in love with Jesus Christ and to live our Carmelite charism more intensely. (Age 38)

To continue to grow in conformity to Christ & allow Him to Love me into the Holiness He intends for me. (Age 31)

In ten years, I hope that our Congregation is still faithful to the teachings of the Church. I pray that we are a community that is filled with gratitude for the blessings the Lord has bestowed on us and that we are ever more deeply rooted in prayer. May we always be women in love with our Lord, Jesus Christ and may our love for Him fuel us with courage to do His will and serve those to whom He calls us. (Age 37)

This generational pattern among the younger entrants to express more hope for growth in holiness and fidelity to the Church was also evident in the quantitative data from the 2019 survey (see table 3.2). The Millennial and Generation Z respondents are more likely than the older respondents to say that the prayer life of their institute had "Very Much" had attracted them and had influenced them to enter it. They are also somewhat more likely to say they were "Very Much" attracted to religious life by a desire to be more committed to the Church.

Table 3.2 Quantitative Survey Responses (USA 2019), by Generation

	Vatican II %	Post-Vatican II %	Millennial %	Gen Z %
Attracted "very much" by the prayer life of the institute	71.2	65.8	76.2	82.6
Influenced "very much" by the prayer life of the institute	72.4	67.4	78.1	86.7
Attracted "very much" by a desire to be more committed to the church	48.3	45.6	47.9	54.3

There are no intergenerational differences in the quantitative survey data for whether the institute's charism had attracted the respondents to their institution or influenced them to enter it. But a subtle difference is revealed in the sisters' open-ended responses about their hopes and concerns for how their institute's charism or mission would be lived in the future. Younger respondents are more likely to mention their hope that their institute *will remain faithful* to its charism and divine call, and that they will continue to follow the traditional model of religious life. The older entrants are more likely to fear that their institute *will not change* in response to new calls. There is also a subtle difference between the younger and the older sisters in how they talk about their charism and the vows: the older sisters are more likely to say they hope to *live* their charism/vows, while the younger ones are more likely to say they hope to *remain faithful* to the charism/vows—which may imply that they think some other institutes have *not* remained faithful. Table 3.3 outlines some of these differences.

Table 3.3 Hopes and *Concerns* about the Future, by Generation

Hope/*Concern*	Vatican II (Age 59+) N=54 N=49 %	Post-Vatican II (Age 39–58) N=235 N=216 %	Millennials I (Age 31–38) N=277 N=259 %	Millennials II (Age 24–30) N=221 N=220 %	Gen Z (Age <24) N=42 N=39 %
Remain faithful to charism/vows	9.3	11.1	25.6	32.1	28.6
Remain faithful to the traditional model of religious life	0	3.4	12.6	10.9	19.0
We will not change in response to new calls	*20.4*	*7.4*	*4.2*	*1.4*	*0*
Live/witness to the charism/vows	16.7	8.5	8.7	12.7	7.1

Samples of these responses include:

In the future, I hope that my community continues in fidelity to the great gift we have been given from our older Sisters. I hope that we continue to live more deeply our consecration to Christ as His Brides and witness to His Love in the Church and the world. (Age 33)

My hopes for the future in my religious institute are that we are faithful to God's will and our charism. I hope we are led by the Holy Spirit and continue to grow in vocations and holiness. While remaining faithful to Mother Church. (Age 28)

I feel that we are riding the waves of change. Similarly to our Sisters who lived in the important changes of Vatican II, we are facing something similar. My concern is that there might be a resistance to welcome the changes that the Spirit might be inviting us to be part of. (Age 39)

That we won't make the big shifts we need to in the next ten years. I worry we are still hanging onto to the past. We talk about going forward together and embracing the unknown future, but I don't see a lot of action behind the words just yet. (Age 35)

As was noted in the quantitative data reported in chapter 2 (figures 2.1 and 2.2), community living is a strong attraction for women entering religious life in the United States today.[2] In listing their hopes for the future of their institute, sisters from the Millennial Generation are the most likely to cite strengthening their institute's unity and community spirit. The very youngest (Generation Z) respondents are somewhat less likely to do so, perhaps because they are still in initial formation and not yet living in local convents. Post–Vatican II and the older Millennial sisters are the most likely to be concerned about divisions and lack of communication as threats to community living. The oldest age groups are the most likely to worry that their institute is attracting too few vocations, and to fear that this will negatively impact community living. A few respondents in the growing institutes fret that attracting too many new members will dilute the community spirit they currently value. In general, older respondents are more likely than younger respondents to favor a diversity of cultures, ages, and socioeconomic statuses among the members of their communities. Table 3.4 summarizes some of these differences.

Table 3.4 Hopes and *Concerns* about the Future, by Generation

Hope/*Concern*	Vatican II (Age 59+) N=54 N=49 %	Post-Vatican II (Age 39–58) N=235 N=216 %	Millennials I (Age 31–38) N=277 N=259 %	Millennials II (Age 24–30) N=221 N=220 %	Gen Z (Age <24) N=42 N=39 %
Strengthen community/ unity/communication	7.4	11.9	16.2	15.4	9.6
Wounded members, divisions, lack communication	0	5.6	3.1	1.8	0
Decreasing community size	6.1	6.0	1.9	3.6	0
Too few vocations	12.2	11.6	6.9	3.2	0
More diversity among members	9.3	10.2	5.4	3.2	2.4

Responses illustrating these hopes and concerns include:

I would like to see the Sisters become more united in mind and heart. I would love to see an importance placed on

---

2. A similar attraction will be noted in Sr. Bibiana Ngundo's chapter (below) among new entrants in Kenya.

praying together in the presence of the exposed Blessed Sacrament. I would also like to see more understanding between generations within our community so that the young sisters feel more welcomed and supported. (Age 35)

Staying healthy in unhealthy situations/systems/relationships. (Age 33)

I am concerned the most of the diminishment, of being the only young person in my community. I am concerned that there will be less viable communities to live in or that I will be living on my own. Community is one of the main reasons why I wanted to enter religious life. (Age 31)

As the community grows, I have concerns about keeping the sense of community which we possess now. We have branched out to serve in countries outside the United States and I am concerned that we might lose our sense of identity as an institute if sisters remain in other countries for years. (Age 34)

Openness to different ways of thinking and acting—more women entering (especially from diverse cultures, socioeconomic backgrounds, and ministerial backgrounds). (Age 31)

That we are able to build ourselves up through additional multi-cultural and multi-economical members. That our order is able to grow in its thinking to focus less on diminishment and more on what it can do today. (Age 47)

Chapter 2 also noted that new entrants in the United States are less likely to be attracted by their institute's mission or ministries (cf. figures 2.2 and 2.7). The two youngest generations are much less likely than the older generations to say that they had been attracted to religious life by a desire to be of service, or to say that their institute's mission was what had attracted them to it (see table 3.5).

Table 3.5 Quantitative Survey Responses (USA 2019), by Generation

	Vatican II %	Post-Vatican II %	Millennial %	Gen Z %
Attracted "very much" to religious life by a desire to be of service	71.7	72.7	59.2	52.2
Attracted "very much" by the mission of the institute	73.3	71.2	57.4	58.7

This pattern was similarly reflected in the answers to the open-ended questions. Ministry is even seen, especially by the younger respondents, as a threat to their religious life, leading to workaholism and a loss of contemplative focus. The youngest cohorts are also concerned about not having adequate training for ministry. The older respondents are somewhat more concerned that the shrinking number of active sisters in their institute may lead to the abandonment of long-standing ministries, while the younger respondents are more likely to express the hope that their institute's ministries will grow and spread to other areas. But these younger respondents seem to see this expansion as primarily involving their current ministry focus, while older respondents are more likely to express a wish to focus more on the needs of the time and the option for the poor. Table 3.6 shows some of these trends.

Table 3.6 Hopes and *Concerns* about the Future, by Generation

Hope/Concern	Vatican II (Age 59+) N=54 N=49 %	Post-Vatican II (Age 39–58) N=235 N=216 %	Millennials I (Age 31–38) N=277 N=259 %	Millennials II (Age 24–30) N=221 N=220 %	Gen Z (Age <24) N=42 N=39 %
Workaholism, loss of contemplative focus	2.0	2.3	2.3	3.6	5.1
Adequate training for ministry	0	0.5	0	4.5	7.7
We won't meet the needs of current ministries	2.0	2.8	2.3	1.8	0
To spread to other areas	0	3.4	7.6	7.2	7.1
To found new convents/missions	0	2.6	5.8	10.9	2.4
Option for the poor	13.0	20.4	11.9	10.9	4.8

Responses illustrating the respondents' concerns include:

> *I guess what most concerns me is that I may be tempted to try to "solve" the needs of the apostolate and become preoccupied with apostolic work without remaining rooted in deep prayers and letting that feed the apostolate. (Age 30)*

> *I worry that I will get burned out with teaching or get too wrapped up in school that my prayer life suffers. (Age 36)*

> *One area [in which] I have concern is that I think it would be helpful if sisters were better trained for the ministries we work in. I don't like the idea of jumping into something I'm not at all prepared for, but this is sometimes how we've had to operate. (Age 35)*

> *That I might be asked to do something that I feel I don't have the skills to do and/or were not prepared for and make someone else's life miserable. (Age 28)*

> *My community has a large population of older members. Even though I know that provisions are being made to take care of these members as they age, I am concerned as to what the future of our apostolate will look like as many of these members enter our nursing home and return to the Lord. (Age 34)*

Other responses illustrate their hopes for the future:

> *We would like to have a convent in Australia. (Age 21)*

> *That we will grow and have more Sisters to send out to all of the Dioceses that are requesting us. (Age 38)*

> *One of my hopes for our community is opening a convent in a developing country in Latin America. I would love to serve the poor in one of those countries. (Age 38)*

> *I hope that our institute will continue to expand and reach as many students in as many schools as possible (we are*

teachers). I hope that we will successfully implement projects to reach out to evangelize using modern as well as traditional media. We have had some success, but there is much more to do. I hope that we will be able to maintain our presence in schools in the face of growing religious opposition in our country's culture. (Age 30)

My hope is that we look at different ways to serve instead of just education/administration. There is a greater need among the elderly/poor, for spreading the Gospel message to so many that don't have a relationship or even an awareness of God. All types of religious formation/education is needed from those in the pew to those who have fallen away from the church. (Age 52)

When looking at the future of their institute, older respondents are the most likely to anticipate its merging with other provinces or with other institutes with the same charism. Sisters from the post–Vatican II and older Millennial generations are the most likely to call for training young members for leadership roles. Both the oldest and the youngest respondents are the most likely to say that they were not concerned at all about the future. There is little consistent generational difference in the percentages of respondents who simply said they are open to whatever God wants for their future. Table 3.7 shows these differences.

Table 3.7 Hopes and *Concerns* about the Future, by Generation

Hope/*Concern*	Vatican II (Age 59+) N=54 *N=49* %	Post-Vatican II (Age 39–58) N=235 *N=216* %	Millennials I (Age 31–38) N=277 *N=259* %	Millennials II (Age 24–30) N=221 *N= 220* %	Gen Z (Age <24) N=42 *N=39* %
Merge/collaborate with other provinces	3.7	2.6	2.2	1.4	0
Manage becoming smaller/diminishment	5.6	6.8	5.8	0.9	0
Train the young for leadership	0	1.7	2.9	0.5	0
Lack of training for leadership	*2.0*	*4.6*	*4.2*	*1.8*	*0*
To be open to whatever God wants	7.4	5.1	6.8	8.1	9.6
I am not concerned at all	*20.4*	*11.1*	*10.0*	*9.1*	*17.9*

Responses listing these hopes and concerns include:

I am hopeful about our becoming one U.S. Province in 2020 and the many opportunities our becoming one will afford us as a religious institute. (Age 47)

I hope my institute will be more connected with other Dominican Institutes. I hope that younger members will have more relationships with members of other institutes. (Age 36)

I'm concerned about the amount of responsibility I'll be asked to assume within the community and whether I'll have the skills, experiences, and time needed to do it while also being able to stay in active ministry/direct service. (Age 38)

I trust in the providence of God, so I do not have concern about the religious life. Although the number of religious have decreased within the decade, I believe in God's will and the Holy Spirit's guidance. The important thing is that religious continue to focus on Jesus and his work and being a witness of the Gospel of Love and allow God to do the rest. (Age 47)

I am not really concerned about my future in the religious life. I plan to make final vows and spend the rest of my life doing God's will as expressed through my superiors. I know the work in the apostolate will be demanding, community life may be bumpy, and mornings will come too early. I also know that the way of life I have chosen is not natural but supernatural. Therefore, I try to keep my eyes on Christ instead of worrying about my future. (Age 24)

Canada

The 2017 Canadian survey of sisters who had entered their institute since 2000 was much smaller than the U.S. survey. Since it was administered two years earlier than the 2019

U.S. survey, the age cutoffs for the Vatican II, post–Vatican II, and Millennial generations were different. In 2017, the Vatican II Generation respondents were over 57 years old, the post–Vatican II Generation respondents were between ages 37 and 56, and the Millennials between ages 22 and 36. The ages in the Canadian tables therefore reflect this difference.

The age distribution of the Canadian sisters was different—and skewed older—than that of the U.S. respondents. Only about 6 percent of the U.S. respondents who answered the open-ended questions were of the Vatican II Generation; 23 percent of the Canadian respondents were. Of the U.S. respondents, 28 percent were of the post–Vatican II Generation, as compared to 48 percent of the Canadians. In the United States, Millennial sisters were by far the largest age cohort at 58 percent of the respondents. In Canada, by contrast, Millennial sisters comprised only 29 percent of those responding to the survey's open-ended questions. There were no Generation Z respondents in the Canadian survey, which is not surprising, since in 2017 that generation was barely 22 years old.

The Canadian survey included three open-ended questions, none of which were the same as those on the U.S. survey:

- What do you find most rewarding or satisfying about religious life?

- What do you find most challenging about religious life?

- What most attracted you to your religious institute?

The remainder of this section will explore generational differences and similarities in the sisters' answers to these questions.

High percentages of all three generational cohorts of women who had newly entered their institutes rank prayer and developing a relationship with God the most rewarding or satisfying aspect of religious life. Younger sisters were more likely to verbalize this relationship as being the spouse of Christ—language that was not at all used by the oldest cohort. The youngest respondents also tend to valorize giving or surrendering all of their life to God, which is less often cited by the older respondents. The youngest respondents are also more likely to list community life as rewarding. The post–Vatican II respondents are the most likely to say that some aspect of their institute's ministry or mission was rewarding. The oldest are more likely to note that religious life offers them ways to grow. Table 3.8 summarizes these findings.

Table 3.8 Rewarding or Satisfying about Religious Life, by Generation

	Vatican II (Age 57+) N=11 %	Post-Vatican II (Age 37–56) N=23 %	Millennial (Age 22–36) N=14 %
Prayer/relationship with God	45.4	56.5	46.7
Giving/surrendering all to God	27.3	17.3	40.0
Community life	27.3	21.7	46.7
Ministry/mission	9.1	34.8	26.7
Opportunities for personal growth and developing talents	18.2	13.0	6.7

Examples of these responses include:

Religious life helps me experience a daily encounter with God, with myself, with others, and with creation. A life of an on-going experience of growth, discovering the mystery of being called to become what God intends me to be. (Age 58)

Giving my life completely over to God for His glory and the salvation of souls; as well as being the spouse of Jesus. (Age 37)

Silence, the intentional silence and personal time to be with God. (Age 34)

The prayer life and the opportunity to deepen my relationship with God. However, that is deepened by the love I experience and give in community and in mission. (Age 29)

Knowing that I'm consecrated to Our Lord and to the Church in a special way, that I'm a Bride of Christ and as such am united to Our Lord in everything I do. (Age 32)

In listing what they found most challenging about religious life, the youngest and the oldest sisters are the most likely to mention difficulties with community living, though some also say it is the most rewarding aspect as well. In this, the Canadian sisters echo the concern of their U.S. counterparts (table 3.4), as well as some of the challenges noted in chapter 8 among the Kenyan sisters. A few of the Canadian sisters specify that the intergenerational or cross-cultural aspects of their community life cause difficulties. The youngest and oldest respondents are also more likely than the post–Vatican II respondents to say that facing one's own faults and limitations is challenging. Younger members are more likely to find challenges in the vow of obedience and letting go of one's own will and preferences. None of the oldest respondents cite this as a challenge; one even said that the vow of obedience was easy and simple to live. Table 3.9 summarizes these findings.

Table 3.9 Challenging Aspects of Religious Life, by Generation

	Vatican II (Age 57+) N=11 %	Post-Vatican II (Age 37–56) N=23 %	Millennial (Age 22–36) N=14 %
Difficulties with community living	54.5	17.4	50.0
Facing one's own faults	18.2	2.2	28.6
The vow of obedience	0	4.3	14.3
Letting go of one's own will/preferences	0	4.3	21.4

Examples of these responses include:

Community living, especially with members of different cultures and intergenerational. But I find this challenge very life-giving, especially in living and witnessing the Word of God among us. (Age 65)

Getting along with other members who are of a different nationality and don't understand our culture of living. This can be extremely frustrating for them and for myself. (Age 46)

My biggest challenge in religious life is dealing with myself and letting myself to become less selfish and giving more of my love to God and others. (Age 37)

Striving to be faithful day in and day out to the will of God, and the will of my Superiors who represent God to me. (Age 31)

The call to give up one's will. (Age 24)

When asked what attracted them to their particular institute, respondents of all generations are the most likely to cite the life and works of the institute's founder or foundress, and his/her charism or spirituality. This response echoes the comparatively higher value candidates placed on the institute's charism as reported in chapter 2 (figure 2.7). While all generations cite prayer and a relationship with God as the most rewarding aspect of religious life, the youngest generation is less likely to list their own institute's prayer or contemplative spirit as something that had attracted them to it. Similarly, although the youngest sisters cite community as a rewarding aspect of religious life (while also admitting it can be the most challenging), this age group is less likely than the post–Vatican II Generation to say it is what had attracted them to their institute. Both the post–Vatican II and the Millennial sisters say they were attracted to their institute by the example of the members and by the wearing of the habit. The post–Vatican II respondents are the most likely to cite their institute's fidelity to the Church and the Magisterium; in the United States, it is the youngest sisters who hope that their institutes will remain faithful to the traditional model of religious life. The youngest Canadian respondents are the most likely to cite the mission or ministry of their institute. In this, they differ from the youngest respondents to the U.S. survey (table 3.5), who are less attracted by their institute's ministry or mission. Table 3.10 summarizes these responses.

Table 3.10 What Attracted the Respondent to Her Institute, by Generation

	Vatican II (Age 57+) N=11 %	Post-Vatican II (Age 37–56) N=23 %	Millennial (Age 22–36) N=14 %
Charism/life of the founder	54.5	43.5	50.0
Its prayer or contemplative spirit	45.5	47.8	28.6
Its ministry or mission	9.1	8.7	42.9
The example of the members	27.3	34.8	35.7
Wearing the habit	9.1	26.1	28.6
Community living	9.1	34.8	14.3
Its fidelity to the church and magisterium	0	21.7	0

Examples of these responses include:

Its charism which are as follows: reparation, adoration and penance. Its ministry, which is prayer, gives me the privilege and opportunity to be in touch with God, with myself, with others and with creation. (Age 58)

Giving all to God through a life of prayer was the first consideration. But meeting the sisters in person and experiencing the way they express community through a live-in really allowed me to witness the authenticity of their joy. (Age 49)

Their fidelity to the teachings and mission of the Church (specifically the Pope and the Bishops in union with him), the wearing of a distinct religious habit, living in Community, and its prayer life. (Age 39)

An interior call to this Order, and also the ministry of the order, the holy and orthodox practice of the community, the

graces I received while first staying with the community, and my experiences living with the community members. Also, religious habit was also very important for me. (Age 24)

Australia

The Australian survey, conducted in 2015, included both male and female religious who had entered their institutes since 2000. A previous survey of the leaders of these institutes had indicated that there were 218 women in formation programs in Australia that year, but only 45 of them responded to the researchers' request to complete the individual survey. The researchers noted that this 20.6 percent response rate meant that there was no way of knowing whether those who answered the survey were representative of those who did not. Of the 45 sisters surveyed, only 38 answered its three open-ended questions. This was even smaller than the 48 respondents who answered the Canadian open-ended questions. Care must therefore be taken in generalizing from these few responses to all of the women who have entered religious institutes in Australia since 2000.

The age distribution of the women responding to the Australian survey fell between the ranges reported for the United States and Canada. Respondents from the Vatican II Generation (born before 1961) comprised 6 percent of the U.S. and 23 percent of the Canadian respondents; 15.6 percent of the Australians were in this age cohort. Comparable figures for the post–Vatican II Generation were 28 percent for the United States, 48 percent for Canada, and 38 percent for Australia. Millennials were the largest cohort responding to the U.S. (58 percent) and Australian (47 percent) surveys, as compared to comprising only 29 percent of the Canadians.

The Australian survey asked the same three open-ended questions that the Canadian survey had asked: what the respondent found most rewarding or satisfying about religious life, what she found most challenging, and what most attracted her to her religious institute. Unfortunately, the ages of each of the 38 respondents to these questions was not given, only whether they were fully professed, temporarily professed, or novices/postulants/candidates. Of these categories, the fully and temporarily professed respondents were more likely (85 percent) to fill out the open-ended questions than the novices/candidates/postulants (73 percent) were.

The low response rate and the fact that the ages of the respondents to the open-ended questions were not reported raise difficulties for analysis. The remainder of this section will assume that the majority of those who responded were of either the post–Vatican II or Millennial generations.[3] It is, of course, impossible to compare generational differences within the Australian sample,[4] so the analysis in this section will compare the Australian responses to the responses of the post–Vatican II and Millennial generations in the United States and Canada.

As with the Canadian survey, prayer and growing in holiness are highly ranked by the Australian respondents as something they find rewarding about religious life. This also corresponds to the younger U.S. respondents' ranking spiritual growth as one of their primary hopes for the future. However, the Australian respondents rank their institute's ministry higher than the respondents in Canada, which corresponds to a similar ranking reported in chapter 2 (figures 2.1, 2.13). Like the Canadian respondents, a minority also cite opportunities for personal growth and developing talents as something they find rewarding. Table 3.11 summarizes these findings.

3. Only one response could definitely be determined to be from an older, Vatican II–Generation respondent; her response is not included in this chapter's analysis.
4. Although one might assume that the fully and temporarily professed respondents would tend to be older than the novices/candidates/postulants.

Table 3.11 Rewarding or Satisfying about Religious Life, by Formation Level

	Finally Professed N=14 %	Temporarily Professed N=14 %	Novices/Candidates/ Postulants N=9 %
Prayer/relationship with God	50.0	21.4	33.3
Growing in Holiness	7.1	35.7	33.3
Community life	50.0	21.4	44.4
Ministry/mission	37.7	42.9	11.1
Opportunities for personal growth and developing talents	7.1	21.4	11.1

Examples of these responses include:

To be with Our Lord in the Blessed Sacrament more often than what is possible in the world. (Temporary vows)

I enjoy the community life and prayer together like the first community in the Bible. All had one heart and everything they shared. The community life is very meaningful for me. Also, that God is growing with me in all aspects and I can answer my call to this congregation. (Novice)

Doing God's will (and in the process finding out who He created me to be). Religious life enables you to find many hidden talents, and to develop many other aspects of one's person that otherwise may never have been used for the glory of God. (Temporary vows)

Again, as with the Canadians (and, as we will see in chapter 8, the Kenyans), the Australians listed community living as the most challenging aspect of religious life. This also corresponds to the American sisters' emphasis on community in their hopes and concerns for the future (table 3.4). Some of the Australians' difficulties with community living, also noted by the American and Canadian respondents, are the age gap between younger and older members, the scarcity of age peers, and intercultural difficulties, but the Australians also cite the difficulty of transitioning from secular life to religious life. Similar to the Americans and Canadians, the younger Australian respondents also cite struggles against their own weaknesses as a challenge in living community. Table 3.12 summarizes these findings.

Table 3.12 Challenging Aspects of Religious Life, by Formation Level

	Finally Professed N=14 %	Temporarily Professed N=14 %	Novices/Candidates/ Postulants N=9 %
Community living	21.4	42.9	33.3
Age gap/no age peers in community	14.3	21.4	22.2
Facing one's own faults	14.3	21.4	22.2
The vow of obedience	0	7.1	0
Being considered a "celebrity"/people expecting too much of me	21.4	7.1	0

Examples of the answers include:

Community life and trying to adapt to the culture of Religious life, as it is so different from the culture of the world that I have been brought up in. (Temporary vows)

The struggle against sin, the day to day fidelity to Him through obedience and docility. Seeking to be open to truth even when it is inconvenient or shows up my many flaws, selfishness and lack of generosity. (Temporary vows)

Living community life in small communities with sisters "set in their ways," controlling, unaware of the other. (Final vows)

False stereotypes and judgments. Community house living with large age and personality differences. (Novice)

As with the Canadian respondents, the charism of the institute and the life of its founder is the major factor which attracted the Australian respondents to their institute, especially for the novices and postulants. The institute's ministry or mission is cited as an attraction by the Australian respondents more often than it is by the older Canadians (or by the Americans in the closed question part of their survey), while the example of its members, its prayer or contemplative spirit, and wearing a habit are cited slightly less often. Community living is a stronger attraction for the older Australian respondents than it is for the Canadians. Table 3.13 summarizes these findings.

Table 3.13 What Attracted the Respondent to Her Institute, by Formation Level

	Finally Professed N=14 %	Temporarily Professed N=14 %	Novices/Candidates/ Postulants N=9 %
Charism/life of the founder	42.9	28.6	66.7
Its prayer or contemplative spirit	14.3	21.4	33.3
Its ministry or mission	28.6	42.9	33.3
The example of its members	14.3	28.6	22.2
Wearing the habit	7.1	14.3	11.1
Community living	21.4	35.7	11.1
Its fidelity to the church and magisterium	0	21.4	11.1

The United Kingdom and Ireland

As was mentioned above in the section on methodology, the 2015 study done in the United Kingdom and Ireland was composed of fifty-three extended, one-on-one interviews and additional written surveys of twelve respondents who did not wish to be personally interviewed. The study differed from the U.S., Canadian, and Australian studies in several other ways: it also included sisters in Anglican institutes and respondents who had entered after 2000 but had since left. For the analysis in this chapter, we will focus only on the responses from the twenty-three Catholic sisters who were interviewed and the two Catholic sisters who completed questionnaires, omitting the Anglican responses and the responses from those who had left. Most of the sisters were from the United Kingdom; nine were from Ireland. As with the Australian survey, the ages of the respondents were not given but can sometimes be inferred from the text of the response. A more extended discussion of the findings of this study will be given in chapter 5.

As with the U.S., Canadian, and Australian respondents, the sisters who had entered institutes in Ireland and the United Kingdom since 2000 frequently cite their appreciation of community and the opportunities which they experience in religious life to grow in holiness, prayer, and their relationship with God. These were by far the most commonly mentioned responses in the interviews:

Well, the reason I wanted to join a community was to have, like, Christ at the centre of my life. I didn't want it to be just like, going to Mass on a Sunday or just part of my life. I felt like life is a bit fragmented, isn't it? And I didn't want it to be just a little box, a little part of me. I wanted it to be the full thing, the thing that everything else in my life springs from and obviously in the monastery I have got that . . . Everything in my life is focused around Christ. (United Kingdom, new member)

As a child, I always felt that you couldn't love somebody you didn't know, so I always wanted to know more, like, to know God more . . . Looking back, I think that what was very important for me would have been the commitment of all of us to seek God, if that makes sense, that Jesus is the most important person. (Ireland, new member)

I think genuinely it is one of the amazing things of religious life, I think, that you can put this random group of women together who probably out of religious life wouldn't be drawn together in any way, shape, or form and it works. Like, somebody once said to me, "How do you know that God exists?" and I said, "You look at religious community because it does . . . like, you get women who are willing to put themselves, not second always, but just put them like, throw themselves into a common project and it works." (United Kingdom, new member)

The days when [sisters] all went to work in school and they all lived together and all lived what they called community and we see [that] as more like of communal living: they just all follow the same schedule, you know? My idea of community would be . . . more about how we relate, the depth of relationship, sharing houses in smaller groups and living and sharing faith. (Ireland, new member)

As the report's authors say, "The ideal of community emerges strongly as one of the major attractions to a religious vocation, even where in reality it proves difficult to live up to. Anyone who has lived religious life over the long term is likely to say that, while life in community is one of the primary ideals, it can also present one of the primary challenges." (Simmonds and Calderón 2020:71). This was reflected in the comments which the sisters made about the challenges they faced in community living:

[T]hey used to have their main meal at lunch time, so I'd kind of come home from work and there would be like three old ladies and the supper would be like a boiled egg and . . . I felt . . . I think I had more community when I was living on my own and had my own kind of networks . . . I felt much more part of community in prayer and . . . those things than I did when I was actually living with a community where the sisters were mostly out in the evening . . . Like even if we went to the same Mass everyone would sit in different places, you know? I am like, "What does it mean to say that you are a community if . . . there's like four people from the community who are at the same Mass and one is over there, one's there,

one's there and one's there and they all . . . walk home separately?" (United Kingdom, new member)

Community life is, of course, difficult, a lot of it is just not being able to have things the way you would want them, you know, like for example having to eat food that I wouldn't necessarily choose or wouldn't choose to prepare in that way or whatever, but I, I guess I think these things are like a means to an end spiritually . . . They are an invitation to me to be less selfish and to kind of learn to accept things, that I am not on my own terms. So, I think community is very fruitful even though it can be incredibly demanding (United Kingdom, new member)

As with the Australians and the Canadians, the Irish and British sisters noted that intercultural gaps—in age, class, and ethnicity—were also challenges to living in community:

It is a different culture . . . I struggled to understand. When I don't understand something, it is harder to obey, to just follow, to do what you are told. . . . That requires acceptance and training as well, to know that there are other ways to do things, people have other ways. It is something I am learning. . . . but I learned in community if I were to . . . let those things control me, I would be miserable every day. (United Kingdom, new member)

I know it is a bit difficult when I have to speak to sisters from other generations because sometimes they don't really know what I am talking about and I don't know what they are talking about because it is just a different kind of background . . . but I think it is a chance for us to be open to it and to learn from each other. Being the young generation here means that I can learn a lot from the old ones because they do have more experience than me and also, I need to give them my availability to share with them what

I have experienced in my life as a young person, from a more modern generation. (United Kingdom, new member)

But to me, I don't think there's many people who are kind of lower class people entering communities. I just don't think there are, and I read a book once and that was saying that in the whole church there is change. Apparently there used to be a lot of Irish immigrants . . . and the church used to be very working class but now it is, the church is more middle class. (United Kingdom, new member)

In Asia, we eat rice with a spoon. It is much quicker but in here you learn that you have to eat with knife and fork because it's the culture . . . in our country we are laughing loudly . . . but in here you have to control your voice, you know, . . . and I am like, "Gosh, to me, you know, this has nothing to do with my vocation, but . . . every time I eat people are looking at me and if I hold it the wrong way, I will get scolded in front of the Novice Mistress." . . . Then after that I have just no appetite to eat anymore." (United Kingdom, new member)

On the other hand, some of the interviewees enjoyed living in communities with older sisters:

Personally, I don't have any difficulties with the . . . elderly sisters because . . . I used to live with my grandparents. All my life . . . I lived with elderly people . . . I got on well with them and again with my sisters in our congregation, I get on well with them as well and of course you have to learn through them . . . because it is a beginning for me. I entered into the congregation where I don't know much about the life of the congregation, so I need them to support me, to teach me, so I take everything what they give me as a lesson, so I don't have any problem at all, thanks be to God. (United Kingdom, new member)

Several of the interviewees mentioned that wearing a religious habit and being in a traditional religious community was attractive to them. This desire was not exclusive to the younger sisters, as it tended to be in the United States, Canada, and Australia. One sister who had entered her congregation when she was in her sixties stated:

I wanted a religious life, which was with a proper veil, a habit, and somebody telling you what to do . . . that was the only kind of religious life I had known. (United Kingdom, new member)

Younger interviewees were more likely to link the habit to giving a visible witness:

One thing I didn't like was that one of the sisters told me that where she worked nobody knew that she was a religious sister. And to me that wasn't really what I wanted. I think that was very common in the past, like it was about being with people and I think people used to think nuns are somehow better and so they were trying to get away from that, and try to blend in. But for me, I was like, "No, I want to be a witness and I want people to know." (United Kingdom, new member).

One of the signs of the times [is] that suddenly the interest in the habit is back and it is a different way of wearing the habit. I know there is a lot of old sisters who are quite allergic to it. You know, they come out of . . . a very strict way of religious life . . . It was also the time that we founded ministries in, in Latin America, this option for the poor, so you could see where they were coming from. And suddenly there is this generation that says, "Now listen, what about the habit?" And they are like super allergic, not realizing that wearing the habit today means something different than wearing it in 1950. (Ireland, new member)

As with the sisters surveyed in the other countries, the British and Irish interviewees cited the witness of the other sisters in their congregation as something that had strongly attracted them to it:

> *I think when I went to the monastery I just found it so refreshing that they were so themselves and just in such a true and honest way and to see it, like you could see their authenticity, you could see kind of their freedom in their silence to Christ, and they were so uninhibited by their life . . . and by talking to them you got the sense they were so real and so down to earth. (Ireland, inquirer)*

> *I think one thing that I hadn't expected was, there is just how much fun we would have together, you know? When we . . . all sat around at recreation after supper and everyone sat behind in the community room just kind of chatting and laughing . . . that was just . . . tremendous fun and I think I wasn't expecting that at all, you know. (United Kingdom, new member)*

> *[An elderly sister with dementia] made a massive impression on me, actually, because the goodness kind of shone through this old woman and she was gentle and kind and she loved God and I mean, it, it is hard to say really what was happening but it was quite clear that when she received communion that, that was everything to her, that was just, her world was . . . receiving communion. . . . It was awe-inspiring, really, I was, I was partially scared to be in the presence of such faith. (United Kingdom, new member)*

Few of the interviewees, however, mentioned being inspired by the sisters' ministries or their work among the poor and marginalized. In this, they were more similar to the U.S. respondents.

The report concluded that women in the United Kingdom and Ireland continue to hear and respond to the call to religious life, and that they are attracted by the sisters' witness of coherent commitment, by prayer and spiritual life lived in community, by charism, and by wholehearted mission. Dealing with age-, class-, and ethnicity-related cultural diversity in community is difficult, but the sisters are finding ways to cope with it. They also have a strong commitment to live simply and in solidarity with the poor (Simmonds and Calderón 2020:17)

France

In addition to the French survey described in chapter 2, thirteen focus groups were conducted: ten of young men and women religious under the age of forty, and three of the more senior religious who were serving as novice directors or other formation personnel in their institutes. Nine of these focus groups were of women religious, and this section will focus on their responses. Since only women religious under the age of forty participated in these focus groups, we can assume that they are roughly of the Millennial and younger post–Vatican II generations, if in fact the generational categories used in U.S. studies apply in France.

Much of the focus-group discussions centered on the lack of knowledge or understanding about consecrated religious life in the larger French public, and on ways that religious institutions might counter misperceptions or ignorance about what vowed religious are and do, so as to attract more young women and men to enter. The responses on this topic will be analyzed in chapter 4. The focus group participants did, however, discuss what had attracted them to religious life and what they found satisfying and challenging.

The great majority of the male and female religious (89 percent) said that they came to religious life because of a call from God, although the age they felt this call and their certitude about it varied:

I had a call, but it was made many times and in a very discreet way.

> *Every road is really unique. Certain people have a vocation when they are 11 years old, and others like Sister Y, never thought about a vocation before she was 27.*
>
> *To love and to serve as a celibate [religious] . . . is a huge risk . . . I therefore put the question aside for several years, yet now today here I am—a Sister.*

As chapter 2 points out, the importance of God's call is similarly cited by the sisters surveyed in Australia, the United States, and Canada.

Also similar to the sisters in all of the other countries, the French sisters found community life attractive (cf. figures 2.1 and 2.2) although, like the sisters in the other countries, they also found it difficult. But rather than citing difficulties due to generational or cultural differences, they focused instead on the need to subordinate one's own preferences to those of others, a difficulty that had also been cited by the Canadian sisters:

> *It is the renunciation of oneself, of one's own will, that is the most difficult.*
>
> *What is the hardest? It is perhaps to renounce oneself when one is taking the lead with a sister, what is hard is to have the humility, to say to oneself, "OK, I will let this go, it isn't important." To realize that one is not right, it is really an interior struggle. And besides, as they say, pride doesn't die until an hour after the person does! We have a lot of trouble to get rid of oneself, of one's pride, of one's will, and I think that there are times when it is not at all easy.*

Like the sisters surveyed in the other countries, the French sisters in the focus groups mentioned the example and the welcoming spirit of their institute's members as something that had attracted them to it:

> *One day, I happened to receive a flier which invited people to a 5-day retreat. . . . Upon opening the envelope, I said*

to myself, *"Why not?"* I had never made a silent retreat and I didn't think a Christian could pray all day like that. That shows the state of ignorance that I had about the Church. . . . I thought I would arrive at an abbey with silent monks, and actually it was . . . a huge celebration! That is perhaps how it began. [I thought] *"if these people are as normal as I, and if they are capable of dancing on a podium to welcome us, it is because they are free,"* and it was their free spirit that touched me.

Again, like the sisters in the other countries, the French sisters found the vows of poverty and celibacy to be freeing rather than restrictive. While they also, at times, found the vow of obedience difficult, they did not interpret it as completely subordinating one's will to another, as the Australian and Canadian respondents had, but rather as a dialogue of discernment:

> *I am not the master of my own life, but I receive it from an Other, and that passes through my sisters, through a mediation. Thus, it comes about through a dialog, because for me listening goes with dialog.*

> *It is interesting that the etymology of the word "obey" means "to hear," and the first thing in the essence [of obedience] is that I hear something, and afterward I do what I want, but what I am going to do is born from the act of hearing. Therefore, obedience is an act of liberty, contrary to what people say.*

> *Obedience liberates us from our own demands and our ego, but its sense is rather to permit us to insert ourselves in a larger mission.*

> *It is not a stupid and blind obedience, it is really an obedience that is active and responsible.*

Compare this with the comments of the youngest Canadian sisters (table 3.9) or the oldest entrant in the UK/Ireland study, quoted above (p. 70).

The other topics covered in the U.S., Canadian, and Australian surveys—wearing a habit, remaining faithful to the traditional form of religious life, ministry among the poor and marginalized—were not mentioned in the report of the focus groups, although they did occur in the French survey analyzed in chapter 2. A theme running through the French report which did not occur in the other countries was that the larger French society had stereotyped all religious as contemplatives and were not aware of apostolic religious institutes. The larger public also tended to value contemplative monasticism negatively, as a refuge from the problems of the world, but they viewed active religious life more positively once they were aware of it.

> *People's beliefs about religion are stuck in a vision of medieval religion, with chastity, obedience which is seen as something very negative, or as if the Church was rejecting the larger society, which is false.*

The sisters in the focus groups spoke of having to combat these negative views, but perhaps they also were influenced by them, since there were no mentions in the report of the worry—often voiced by the younger U.S. sisters—that their active ministry would detract from their contemplative focus.

Conclusion: Similarities and Differences across Generations and Countries

The social locations of generation, nationality or ethnicity, and social class do influence whether women are attracted to religious life, the kind of religious institute they choose to enter, and what they expect or hope for in their vocation.

Across all countries, the women who have entered religious institutes since 2000 are responding to a deeply felt spiritual call. They all value the opportunities afforded by religious life to center their lives on prayer and to grow closer to God. Also, across all countries, the newly entered sisters value living, working, and praying in common with other members of their institute, although they realize it is often problematic. The difficulties vary, however: The Canadian, French, and Australian sisters are more likely to mention giving up one's own will and preferences as a difficulty. The Australian, English, Irish, and Canadian sisters cite difficulties arising from cultural clashes between sisters of different ages, classes (in the United Kingdom), and ethnicities, while, in contrast, the older U.S. sisters express a desire to have more ethnic diversity in their institutes. Ministry is differently valued by sisters in different countries and by sisters in different generations: the youngest U.S. and Australian sisters worry about spending too much time in ministry to the detriment of contemplation and prayer, a concern that is not cited in other countries. In some countries, it is the older generation of newly entered sisters who were attracted to their institute by its ministries; in other countries, it is the younger sisters who were attracted by their institute's ministries.

One key difference specifically noted in the report of the Australian study is that the newer members of religious institutes in the United States seem to be more divided by theological and ideological differences than the newer members in Australian religious institutes. In the U.S. survey, this is especially reflected in the hopes and concerns which the various generations of respondents express (see tables 3.1 and 3.2), with the younger respondents more likely to fret that their institute might drift away from loyalty to the Magisterium and the traditional model of religious life. This ideological difference "was never mentioned by the new members" in Australia, "either in the open-ended comments made in response to the New Members' Survey or in the focus groups. This may indicate that there is less polarization among religious in Australia than in the United States" (Dixon et al. 2018:58). Similarly, the younger and older new entrants to religious institutes in the United Kingdom and Ireland do not differ in their desire to wear a religious habit or belong to a traditional model religious community, in contrast to the generational differences noted in the U.S. survey.

A strength of religious life over the two millennia of the Church's history has been its wide variety. Each founder's charism responded to a specific time, place, and need. The vision and preferences of new entrants to today's institutes are another example of this.

4

Obstacles to Vocation Discernment and Entrance

Chapter 3 described the responses to the open-ended survey questions by women who had entered religious institutes in Australia, Canada, France, Ireland, the United Kingdom, and the United States since 2000 and were still members. A 2012 Center for Applied Research in the Apostolate (CARA) study of Catholic women and men in the United States had found that a surprisingly large percentage—23 percent of Vatican II women, 8 percent of post–Vatican II women, and 7 percent of Millennial women—had considered religious life at some point in their lives (Gray and Gautier 2012:2). Until the mid-twentieth century, far more women than men acted upon this early consideration and entered religious institutes (Wittberg 1994:31–40). Today, however, numerous studies have found that many young adults are leaving Catholicism altogether, or are reducing their affiliation and participation to only nominal levels (Gray 2011; Smith et al. 2014; McCarty and Vitek 2017; Saad 2018; Bullivant 2019). And for the first time in centuries, fewer women than men among young adults remain active Catholics, which has obvious implications for their willingness to consider a religious vocation (D'Antonio et al 2013; Pew 2019; Burge 2020). This chapter will explore some of the reasons that the national studies examined in this book have given for why few women enter religious institutes today, and what suggestions have been made to attract more.

The studies use different methodologies to address this question and cannot be easily compared. The 2019 U.S. survey included an open-ended question, "What are the greatest obstacles in vocation discernment for discerners and vocation directors?" This question was answered by women religious who had entered their institutes since 2000. Some of these respondents had only recently joined their institute and were still postulants or novices; others had been members for a decade or more and were now vocation or formation directors themselves. The Australian study did not address the question of obstacles to vocation discernment in its survey of new members, but it did survey and interview current institute leaders who raised the topic. The study done in the United Kingdom and Ireland interviewed fifty-three women who had entered religious institutes (some of whom had since left), but it also included interviews with institute leaders and formation and vocation personnel, along with a focus group of theologians and other experts. The French study took a different approach: in addition to interviewing newly entered religious men and women, it also included an online survey, conducted by a professional research organization, of one hundred French adults, in order to surface the impressions that the general public in France had of religious life.

While the methodologies of the studies differed, their conclusions were often quite similar. Many of the respondents, interviewees, and focus-group members mentioned external conditions and influences in the larger society, in the Church, and among the women's relatives and friends as posing obstacles to discerning a religious vocation. A second frequently cited factor was various obstacles in the institutes themselves: the age gap between the current sisters and the potential entrants, difficulties and deficiencies in an institute's formation program, and the sisters' failure or reluctance to invite new members. A third factor—cited primarily in the U.S. survey—pertained to characteristics of the discerners themselves: their immaturity, their lack of familiarity with or their idealization of religious life, and their financial debts due to the high cost of their college education. Each of these obstacles will be examined in turn.

External Factors

As the previous chapter has pointed out, human beings are influenced by the environment of their early childhood as they choose their adult path in life. This environmental background is thus a key factor in whether a young adult will consider entering a religious institute.

The larger secular culture, first of all, exerts a profound influence. Both the U.S. and the Australian respondents point to the numerous distractions and busyness of modern society, which has reduced the time and the capacity for silence, reflection, and prayer. This is the second-most often cited obstacle by the U.S. sisters. Many of the key values of secular culture are cited by the respondents as actually being antithetical to those of the Church. In addition, several of the respondents in the United States, Australia, the United Kingdom, and Ireland note that there are many more options for women today than there were sixty or seventy years ago.

> *I think the greatest obstacle for discerners is emotional stimulation—the constant temptation to fill the void, to drown out the silence, to find satisfaction in transient pleasures, to never allow God to speak in the uncomfortable silence of our own inadequacy. (United States, survey response)*

> *I think some of the greatest obstacles today for discerners can be fear and social media/technology which has become*

> very addicting and many rely on it for security, relying on it for their safety, instead of God, it is harder to hear His voice with all the distractions of the world today. (United States, survey response)
>
> There is so much good young people can do as laypeople. Yet there has to be a difference, a sign of something more, that attracts youth to religious life. We need to question ourselves: what is the difference that we bear witness to? (Australia, focus group)
>
> I believe that there are so many options for women in today's world. There are also more opportunities to live in community besides religious communities. (United States, survey response)
>
> [I left my institute because I went] from the wonderful time I had with [the sisters] and being able to be me and to find myself, to knowing that I could live as a person of faith, spirituality outside the congregation. (Ireland, former member, interview)

Another problematic aspect of the surrounding culture in which Catholic young adults passed their childhood and adolescence is the lack of any chance to meet sisters and get to know them—or even to see them at all. This difficulty is mentioned by both new entrants and vocation personnel in the United States, the United Kingdom, Ireland, and France. As the final report of the United Kingdom and Ireland survey noted, "In Ireland, which was formerly considered a 'Catholic country' where the prevailing culture was deeply embedded in the majority Catholic faith, it is no longer possible to assume that young people have any effective connection with the Church or with religious at all" (Simmonds and Calderón 2020:88).

> Although I was raised Catholic and attended Catholic school from preschool through college, I experienced a

lack of exposure to religious life that resulted in not thinking of it as a possibility and not having an accurate picture of what it is. I would say that was the biggest obstacle for me. (United States, survey response)

Since we no longer have a strong presence in institutions (e.g., schools, hospitals) and are no longer as visible to the world (without wearing habits), it is more difficult to show people that religious sisters are still around and doing good things. We need to find new ways of encountering young women and giving public witness to the beauty of modern religious life. (United States, survey response)

Feedback at career fairs and from guidance counsellors is that students today do not know anything about sisters and religious life. Most have not even met a sister. (United Kingdom, vocation promoter, interview)

I think one of the things I, I fear is that religious, especially the religious women, have lost their place in the church structure, you know. We are not part of the church really . . . we are almost invisible in the church structure . . . we are not there . . . If people don't see that there is this life, they are not going to be attracted by it. (United Kingdom, new member, interview)

Lacking the personal experience of getting to know women religious, young people fall back on depictions of them in the media, which are often negative or off-putting. The online survey of the larger French public found that their general image of Catholic women religious was drawn almost completely from media depictions that portrayed sisters as stunted persons who live "walled-up" in a monastery, "fleeing from the difficulties of daily life." Few even seemed aware that there *were* women religious who were actively ministering in the larger society. This was, the survey said, due to "their lack of visibility—a smaller and smaller number of men and women religious, apostolic religious who are rarely visible or recognizable, a lack of connection with the population at large, outside of big events . . . which doesn't allow the larger public to understand who they are and what they do" (*Attractivité et évolution* 2016:13).

The United States media often presented a different, but equally negative, depiction of sisters:

> *Our public image is one of aging sisters in wheelchairs. While it is inspiring to see these elderly sisters who have served their whole lives, I think young people need more positive, uplifting images/stories of sisters that are active and making a difference—showing them in ACTIVE ministry and having fun/laughing/praying. (United States, survey response)*

In addition to the obstacles posed by the media and society in general, the Church itself poses problems for women discerning entrance into a religious institute. Respondents in the United Kingdom and Ireland, as well as in the United States, mention the impact of Church scandals and some of its teachings on sexuality:

> *Sometimes the Church will come out with something and you think, "Oh, my God." And you somehow feel that you are part of the Church because you, you know, you formally have a role in the Church and yet you really disagree with . . . around the scandal of the sex abuse by priests, you know, it is just very difficult to kind of tread that wire between, between saying . . . "I disagree with this completely," and yet continuing to be faithful to the Church. (United Kingdom, new member, interview)*
>
> *Many questions of young people—committed to their faith and to a life given for others—who struggle with the*

Church's position on or response to issues that are key for them: women's role in the Church, sexuality/non-heterosexual unions, use of power. A vocation in and of the Church is difficult to embrace by those who I do believe may have vocations to this life. (United States, survey response)

Others mention a lack of support for vocations from their local diocese or parish, and the paucity of information about sisters in Catholic schools:

My home diocese had a vocation office, but it focused almost exclusively on men's vocations to the priesthood. Its website had pages and pages for men discerning their vocation and nothing for women (just a page with a listing of the communities of sisters in the area). When I called, I was told to look at the Vision website, which I'd already seen. In short, I received no help whatsoever. This diocese is not alone in ignoring women's vocations. (United States, survey response)

I really wanted to, to do something for God and to live my life for Him and maybe that would transpire into a vocation but I didn't know how to articulate that and I didn't know what you were supposed to do at all, like at the time I didn't know any priests personally . . . Like you have to do, you have to research that and learn yourself to do it. (Ireland, inquirer, interview)

As far as the bishops are concerned, which is the feedback from young people as well as from my experience, they are mostly eager to promote priesthood rather than religious life. So, where the normal experience of a Catholic in the church would be to go to their parish priest for help, when it's somebody thinking about religious life or . . . anything vocational, it is difficult for them to find the next place to go. (United Kingdom, vocation promoter, interview)

Another Church-related obstacle to discernment, cited primarily by the U.S. survey respondents and the interviewees in the UK/Ireland surveys, is the lack of theological and prayer formation among Catholic youth, even among those who had gone to Catholic schools.

Not knowing how to pray or have a relationship with God and not having silence in their life is also a struggle. (United States, survey response)

Women come with various theological backgrounds. Some only have Mass experience, some with CCD, some with a deeper relationship with God. (United States, survey response)

People say: "Do what you want. God shows you what He wants by putting the desire in your heart." . . . So, I guess the greatest obstacle for me was the absence of clear rules of discernment. (United States, survey response)

I used to meet with a sister for kind of spiritual direction and she really introduced me to silent prayer, which I hadn't really encountered before. (United Kingdom, new member, interview)

Finally, many respondents cite discouragement by family and friends as an obstacle to discerning a vocation to religious life:

My mum's immediate reaction was, "How could you even consider such a thing?" That hurt, and then I couldn't say anything. I just kept quiet. I couldn't say anything. I was back for one month; for one whole month we did not speak about it at all, no, not at all. I think she didn't know how to deal with it, so our relationship wasn't that good. We didn't talk about it; she pretended it didn't happen. (United Kingdom, new member, interview)

My dad is an atheist, they didn't really say anything about becoming Catholic, but when I decided to enter the monastery that was a different thing, he wasn't very happy about that. He said, "Oh, you might as well be in prison, you are just wasting your life." But he's OK now. (United Kingdom, new member, interview)

Parents. They too often discourage their children from pursuing their vocation, despite having shown encouragement and support for it in a general way prior to discovering that their own child received a call. Young people are less independent from their parents these days, therefore making their opposition very difficult to overcome. (United States, survey response)

Fear of parental disapproval sometimes makes discerners hesitate even to broach the topic of vocational discernment with their parents:

The greatest obstacle in my life to my vocation was my parents' adamant opposition to my vocation. I had a very close relationship with them, and so I tried not to pursue the call and kept silence about it for many years because I didn't want to hurt my relationship with them. . . . I wonder how many vocations are thwarted because of lack of parental or familial support. (United States survey response)

I was very close to my parents, my worry was not to hurt them, because it was a rather radical step. I have three brothers but I am the only daughter, with all the emotional questions that come from that. Therefore, I said to myself, "This is going to be a catastrophe, it will not go well." My greatest worry was my family. (France, new member, interview)

Some respondents also report that thinking about a religious vocation was a taboo subject among their friends, even at Catholic schools:

> *In secondary school I never heard religious vocation suggested as a possibility. I went to [Convent] Secondary School . . . but it wasn't, it isn't presented now. . . . The problem with suggestion in school is, from my experience . . . the pressure not to be interested is significant. . . . there is a huge kind of pressure within the school not to be interested in God from the other students, if that makes sense, you know? (Ireland, new member, interview)*

> *One great obstacle is a lack of support from other young people. I was seen as old-fashioned and a bit taboo when I told my friends I was discerning. The attitude is "Are nuns still even around anymore?" among many young people today. (United States, survey response)*

In the Australian survey of new members, only one-third or fewer of the sisters report receiving "very much" encouragement from their parents (33 percent), their friends (31 percent), their siblings (27 percent), people in their workplace or school (11 percent), or diocesan priests (22 percent). Even after entering, fewer than half of the women religious responding report receiving very much encouragement from their relatives or friends (Dixon et al. 2018:46).

Unlike in previous centuries, therefore, a young woman discerning a religious vocation receives little support from the larger culture, from her relatives and friends, or even from the Church itself. As the report on the United Kingdom and Ireland survey put it, "Exploring a religious vocation emerges as a far more isolated and lonely business than in the past, with obvious support structures few and far between" (Simmonds and Calderón 2020:30).

Institute Factors

In addition to the obstacles posed by the larger culture, the Church, and the discerner's own family, other obstacles stem from the institutes themselves. Primary among these is the age gap between an institute's present membership and young women discerning a religious vocation. The young adults in the various studies are, understandably, reluctant to join an institute whose members were all several decades older. Both the newly entered sisters and the sisters in leadership, vocation promotion, and formation ministry note that the age gap affects relations between the members. As the report of the Australian study put it, "Several congregational leaders reported during their interviews that age differences between those who had been in the congregation for a long time and the new members could be a source of conflict and tension. They said it was a challenge to integrate new members into a community where the existing members had long-standing relationships, especially when there were very few new members" (Dixon et al. 2018:32). At times, this affects the quality of the formation that the young sisters received.

> *[One obstacle is] the lack of younger women to give energy, new life, and hope to our community. The aging sisters are full of wisdom and love, but having a large number of them means a lot of time and energy is spent caring for them . . . [It is also challenging] being the youngest in the community. (Australia, survey response)*

> *At times, it feels like formation directors do not understand the needs of the young because they are often more than 30–40 years older than us. (United States, survey response)*

> *Another challenge is the meeting of those who have only known religious life and those just moving into this lifestyle. We are both coming from very different aspects of life. (Australia, survey response)*

In addition to the difficulties posed for the institute by the age gap, which is cited by both the newly entered sisters and the vocation personnel and leadership, there are other institute factors mentioned by the women who were still in formation. Several note that their institute has had so few entrants for so long (or had had none at all) that they no longer have an adequate formation program:

> When I asked about going forward [in formation] she said that I was not ready and I knew I was not ready because I was not being taught anything. . . . That was the problem and a community who is in that situation should perhaps think twice before accepting a person if there's any doubt at all whether or not they would be able to provide sufficient training and instruction for that person. (United Kingdom, inquirer, interview)

> There was no sense of understanding where, you know, the younger generation is coming from, there was no sense of formation. I think there was a certain sense of . . . I don't know, they were not prepared, they were not prepared for bringing in new people. (United Kingdom former member, interview)

> Formation programs that slip back into old ways of being and thinking. Vocation directors are often great—but then they have to pass their discerners on to older, often not-well-trained (if trained at all) formators. It's difficult to get people involved in welcoming discerners. (United States, survey response)

> Having formation along an organic style is very different from the military style formation that happened many years ago. "Generation Gap" has returned! (Australia, survey response)

These difficulties will be further discussed by Sr. Ellen Dauwer in chapter 10.

A third factor is alluded to in the responses: apathy among the current members. This affects their willingness either to invite young women to consider a religious vocation or to accept and train for the roles of vocation or formation director.

> No one volunteers for directorship. Those that are most suitable and talented for directorship don't want it and are not tapped. (United States, survey response)
>
> No one wants to step up and help, but they want vocations to come to us. (United States, survey response)
>
> Reluctance to invite newer members to vocation/formation ministry & lack of energy to joyfully invite/engage enquirers. (United States, survey response)
>
> I keep saying to them, "Let's try to do something, let's try and reach out." No interest whatsoever, no energy whatsoever. All we get is messages of people just wanting to connect and being with us and I am having to, like, beg people to get in touch with these people. (United Kingdom, focus group)

The report from the UK/Ireland survey noted that it was not always clear why this reluctance existed, "but it would seem that for some congregations which have not had an applicant for many years, there is a sense of bewilderment and a lack of confidence when faced with someone new wishing to explore a vocation" (Simmonds and Calderón 2020:24).

A final institute factor, mentioned by several in leadership and formation ministry, is the lack of available and healthy community-living situations that could welcome new members:

> Finding thriving communities able to welcome new members and engage at the level that's needed for formation. (United States, survey response)
>
> Healthy welcoming communities. Meeting new members' desire for community. (United States, survey response)
>
> Some young people found when visiting communities that there was no sense of community. The sisters did not pray together, and the only community experience seemed to

be watching TV . . . Some young people were asking why some sisters live alone yet the congregation says community life is important. (United Kingdom, vocations promoter, interview)

As chapter 3 has already pointed out, a desire for community living is one of the main factors that attract new entrants to religious institutes.

The Discerners Themselves

A final obstacle, cited primarily by the U.S. respondents, stems from perceived deficiencies in the young adults themselves. These include fear of commitment (the most commonly mentioned obstacle in the U.S. survey), immaturity, coming from a dysfunctional or wounded family background, individualism, and an overidealized picture of religious life.

I think that the greatest obstacles in vocational discernment for discerners are a fear of commitment and immaturity regarding living in community, taking personal responsibility, and working toward the common good. (United States, survey response)

I think the greatest obstacles come from our culture that seems to instill a fear of commitment. Young people seem to want to keep all their options open and to approach what they do with their lives from what they think will "fulfill" them, instead of asking the questions, "What does God want? Why did He make me?" I think helping them see that total, irrevocable self-gift in a vocation is possible and desirable is the greatest challenge to vocation directors today. (United States, survey response)

Our culture teaches us to be extremely self-centered and focused on "self-fulfillment." It is necessary to overcome the mindset and its corresponding sense of entitlement. I think many young people today find it difficult to be obedient and to work hard, when they have been raised in such a culture. It is difficult to freely and wholeheartedly make a total gift of yourself—or even take the "risk" of entering an institute—in a culture where such a choice cannot be understood. (United States, survey response)

As the vocation director for our community I have a lot of people come to me who have mental health issues, physical health issues, or other social or maturity issues. I wonder sometimes if they come to me because they have been rejected elsewhere. I wonder if more qualified candidates really consider us. (United States, survey response)

Accepting young people who are willing to be taught. Many young women come in these days thinking they know what religious life is and they are here to tell us where we are wrong and how they know better. (United States, survey response)

While such comments come primarily from the U.S. respondents—both those who have recently entered their institute and those who have been members long enough to be serving in leadership or vocation/formation ministry themselves—problems with the discerners themselves are sometimes mentioned by respondents in other countries. The report of the UK/Ireland survey noted that there were "comments from congregational leaders and formators about their difficulties in dealing with new entrants whom they identify as inflexible and unwilling to adapt to a community setting not tailor-made to suit their personal preferences" (Simmonds and Calderón 2020:92–93). Interviews with institute leaders in the Australian study also cite individualism and not being willing to limit use of social media.

Unique to the United States, however, is an additional obstacle: the burden of student college debt. This last obstacle is among the top ten cited in the U.S. survey, but is not mentioned at all by respondents in other countries.

> Because I had a student loan barrier, I could not formally enter for nearly three years—this is enough time for someone to lose heart and their vocation. During that time of waiting, it was necessary for me to fundraise (through the Labouré Society) to completely mitigate my student loan barrier before I could enter religious life. (United States, survey response)

Another issue unique to the United States is the country's immigration regulations, which sometimes prevented prospective entrants from joining the institutes, or from remaining in the country long enough to complete their formation.

> I also think we are allowing U.S. immigration laws to limit us and, again, denying those who are answering God's call.
>
> Discerners from foreign countries—VISA, etc. . . .

Suggested Remedies

The Australian study included a separate survey of fifty-nine leaders of women' religious institutes, and specifically asked about their institute's vocation and formation programs. From the responses to this survey, eight institutes that had attracted and retained at least ten new members since 2000 (three men's institutes and five women's institutes) were selected and interviewed by a member of the research team. The goal of both the Australian survey and the interviews was to compare the vocation and formation practices of the selected institutes to those used by the other institutes. The UK/Ireland study included interviews with three institute leaders and four sisters involved in vocation and formation ministries—again, specifically to assist institutes "to adopt the most effective approaches possible to the promotion and formation of religious vocations."

The other countries' studies did not ask about specific vocation or formation practices. However, the U.S. study did ask the newer members it surveyed (some of whom had been in their institutes long enough to have served in vocations ministry), "What are the greatest obstacles in vocation discernment for discerners and vocation directors?" While most of the answers to this question focused on obstacles to discerners, a subset did mention the difficulties which vocation directors experienced. And both the U.S. and the French studies asked the newer members what was the most helpful in their discernment. From the newer members' list of helpful aids, one can glean recommendations for institute practices.

The first set of recommendations pertains to the institutes themselves. As has been noted in preceding sections of this chapter, young Catholics today have fewer opportunities even to see women religious, let alone become familiar with their lives. The same is true in reverse: many of the respondents note that the sisters themselves are not familiar with the culture of young people. Some respondents say that institutes need actively to educate their older members about their own need to change and adapt to the newer members.

> *Community members struggle with how to talk with young people today. They are fearful of having to enter into discussion with the young people who may have had sexual experiences or have questions regarding pornography. Communities are also fearful about the IT and social media experience of young people. (United Kingdom, vocation minister, interview)*
>
> *So we have to work a lot with the people inside the communities to convert them, make them open to something that is different and also understand . . . the differences within cultures . . . Today's culture and tomorrow's culture*

is radically different, so to begin to open up people's minds and tell them in a logical, in a practical way, "This is how it's different," and . . . when I have been talking to my own sisters in my own community and I have been explaining some of these things, they are actually really enthusiastic about it. It is as if you have given them a key to understanding something. (United Kingdom, vocation minister, interview)

I am a vocation director. My biggest obstacle is encouraging the sisters to think outside our diminishment since most religious articles focus on it. Then for the sisters to be excited about new contacts. (United States, vocation minister, survey response)

The respondents in several studies emphasize the importance of having and supporting an active vocation ministry. While all of the five women's institutes in Australia that had attracted more than ten entrants since 2000 had a vocation ministry, fewer than half of the other institutes did (Dixon et al. 2018:23). While the specific structure of these ministries and personnel varied, all of the five institutes were "highly focused on insuring that the vocations director or team have the support of the community and are resourced accordingly" (Dixon et al. 2018:23–24). The vocations directors in these institutes were twice as likely to be engaged in this ministry full-time rather than part-time. Similarly, several U.S. respondents stated that having a full-time vocation director was essential:

[An obstacle is] discernment directors/vocation directors who aren't well-trained or prepared—especially since given the reality of younger people today, some discerners might have mental health challenges, identify in some way as LGBTQ+, come from difficult/non-supportive or even traumatic family backgrounds. Or vocation directors who wear multiple hats (vocation director AND novice direc-

tor AND archivist AND . . . for example) so can't devote the needed time and energy to accompanying discerners. (United States, survey response)

The French study agreed that "persons trained in accompanying [the discerner] and who know how to answer their questions and guide them" are absolutely necessary (*Attractivité et évolution* 2016:53).

Given the importance of having a full-time, trained vocations minister who is strongly supported by the members and leadership of her community, what activities should she/they engage in? A common thread, according to the Australian focus groups, was "that congregations ought to provide numerous and varied opportunities for members of the community to engage with young people, actively interact with them, and invite them to assist in the community's ministry or join in a community activity" (Dixon et al. 2018:53). This was true in the other studies as well.

Our community tries to be present at various events for young people in the archdiocese. We also attend and speak at retreats/conferences sponsored by the archdiocese in addition to hosting two vocation retreats each year (with a maximum of eight participants in each). In the past we have established a discernment group to assist young women who are discerning. This was successful as young women entered not just our congregation but others, as well as discernment toward marriage. (Australia, vocation minister, interview)

As individual communities, we really need to make that extra effort to go to the people, rather than to have them come to us. To go onto college campuses, to go to where we know there would be a good group of young people that we can witness to. I think many of us have said we didn't see sisters until we were in college, so to make the effort to be seen in the world. (United States, new member, focus group)

> Vocation promotion is an area that all members and communities take very much to heart. We are conscious that the first form of vocation promotion is witnessing of our lived consecrated apostolic life. These are some of the initiatives: days of prayer, taking part in parish/diocesan youth gatherings and vocation expos, inviting young people into our communities for moments of prayer and a shared meal, sharing the stories of our vocations in schools and parishes, personal accompaniment and spiritual direction to those discerning, etc. (Australia, vocation minister, interview)
>
> Many vocations come out of being in relationship with someone from religious life. One of the obstacles with aging and diminishment is that there are less sisters who are in relationship with young discerners. If we do not look at different ways of using technology and be more creative more than just Vision and Facebook, it is difficult to make our congregation and charism more known. (United States, new member, survey response)
>
> Prioritize points of contact: group meetings, immersion experiences, events, discussions . . . (Attractivité et évolution 2016:24)

One common recommendation was to offer "Come and See" experiences. These could vary from simple invitations to join a local community for prayer and a meal or for a special occasion; to spending a week or longer living with sisters in an institute community; to longer, more structured programs involving regular participation in an institute's prayer times or apostolic ministries. The Australian study found that all of the sisters' institutes which had ten or more entrants offered such "Come and See" experiences, in comparison to only two-thirds of the other institutes (Dixon et al. 2018:27). Almost three-fourths (72 percent) of the new members interviewed in the French study said that spending time with the sisters in their homes was a great help in their discernment (*Attractivité et évolution* 2016:36).

> "Come and See" weekends and the retreat gave young people the opportunity to see, meet and talk to people without feeling pressured to join. Young people are highly idealistic and the "Come and See" weekends provide them with an opportunity to talk and discuss. (Australia, vocation minister, interview)

> "Come and See!" But I would rather want to say to congregations "Open Your Doors," bring in young people so that they can see how your communities live, and not just communities elsewhere. (France, new member, interview)

> There was especially one sister who accompanied me on the [discernment] road for an entire year. She said to me, "Come when you want." During a year, I would go every 15 days or once a week to Vespers; I would go there Sunday evenings, I would eat with them. (France, new member, interview)

The studies agreed that it was important to have "an alive and credible web presence," as the United Kingdom report (Simmonds and Calderón 2020:97) described it. The Australian study noted that other forms of social media were also important: 78 percent of the institutes they had selected for interviews because of their success in drawing new members used social media as a promotional tool, as compared to only 28 percent of the other institutes (Dixon et al. 2018:25). But as necessary as websites, the internet, and social media are, both the new members and the vocation ministers say they were not sufficient by themselves.

> I know that some of my sisters looked up [our institute] on the internet, but as for me, I needed words that were real words, and the internet is virtual. (France, new member, interview)

Another way of meeting young adults, forming discernment groups, is cited as very helpful by new members in several countries, but the United Kingdom and Ireland study warns that "group activities requiring a regular commitment are no longer working well with a generation used to making decisions about how to spend their time on the spur of the moment" (Simmonds and Calderón 2020:88).

> *Vocations promotions processes based on regular commitment of a weekend a month or a meeting every few weeks over a year are having less success with a generation averse to making even such regular time commitments as these. (Simmonds and Calderón 2020:105)*

All of these activities, however, take time, and even a full-time vocations minister or team must prioritize which ones are the most important to undertake. As several respondents to the United States survey note:

> *For vocation directors, there are so many events and one-time encounters and a lack of quality of relationships and time versus quantity. (United States, new member, survey response)*

> *There is a danger for vocation directors to also get caught in the numbers game that many in ministry can be distracted by, e.g., number of events, number of interested parties. While metrics are important and there should be objective methods to choose events, there also needs to be openness and sensitivity to the Holy Spirit to place us at events/locations where it might not seem fruitful at the time. (United States, new member, survey response)*

Conclusion

As was noted in the introduction, religious life has existed in the Catholic Church for millennia. In every age, there are people who desire to pursue a deeper relationship with God, strengthened by the presence of others who have a similar desire. In some ages and some countries, this desire leads people to withdraw to a monastic life of prayer and focus on the divine; at other times people are moved to serve Christ in the poor, the sick, and the marginalized. While many obstacles exist, the United States, Canada, France, Australia, the United Kingdom, and Ireland today are no different in having at least some women and men with similar spiritual hungers. The key is finding how to make entering religious institutes a visible and attractive option for young adult Catholics today.

5

New Vocations and Vocational Exploration in Britain and Ireland

Recent statistics regarding religious vocations in the global North have been discouraging. While reports note an increase in the number of Catholics worldwide since the millennium, the number of religious sisters worldwide has decreased by 9 percent. Significant increases in the number of sisters in Asia and Africa have been offset by dramatic decreases in Europe and North America. Conflicting and sometimes contradictory reasons are given for these figures, but most debates about the demographic crisis exclude the voice of vocational seekers themselves. The invitation of that voice into this conversation enables the formulation of vocations promotion and formative programs in dialogue with the lived experience of those who are still seeking a future in religious life.

The following reflection is based on a qualitative research study from 2017 among women who have explored their vocation in Catholic and Anglican religious congregations in the United Kingdom and Ireland since 2000 (Simmonds and Calderón 2020). While it is impossible to capture objective reality through such research, their narratives allow for insight into their experience. Whatever the outcome of their exploration, the narrators offer rich and vital data on what today's generation of entrants is seeking and finding in religious life. Their stories, combined with reflections from formators and leaders of congregations on their experience of receiving new members, form the core of this study, based on open-ended interviews with the data subsequently analyzed using a narrative-analysis approach. It tells of the experience of Catholic and Anglican women's call to religious life and the challenges they have faced in attempting to become part of a community. In some cases, entrants subsequently decided or were asked to leave the community they had joined. The initial intention was to have as many Irish participants as British, but there were difficulties gaining the support of Irish congregations. Some of this was due to distance, the research team being based in the UK, and to an internal reorganization of congregational leadership in Ireland, which had commissioned similar research on the fall of vocational numbers in Ireland, making congregations understandably reluctant to repeat the process. Public perceptions of religious life and the Church in general in Ireland at the time also made some participants and congregations reluctant to come forward, but the nine sisters living in Ireland who were willing to be interviewed offered some thought-provoking and helpful data. In total the study was based on fifty-three in-depth interviews of women who had entered religious life since 2000. Fourteen of those interviewed were Anglican and thirty-nine Catholic, at various stages of religious life. Three (one Anglican, two Catholic) had been or were still seeking; twenty-seven were new members (four Anglican, twenty-three Catholic) and twenty-three had entered religious life and subsequently left (nine Anglican, fourteen Catholic). Others, unwilling to be interviewed, were willing to answer a questionnaire with open-ended questions related to their experience of religious life.

   In narrative research, people look back on an experience and organize it into a meaningful whole through telling a story which bears the imprint of the narrator's interpretation (Chase 2005). The congregations joined or explored by the project's participants initially had no voice in the project, but this risked a serious bias within the overall perspective of the report. Consequently, congregational leaders, vocations promotors, and formators were also interviewed to balance the voices heard within the narratives of new members and of leavers. All personal and identifying references were removed from the interviews and only the research team had access to the raw data. In the final full report, quoted narrators were identified only by letter codes denoting their denomination (or in the case of Irish respondents, who were all Catholic, their nationality), their current status, and a number.

It was decided not to focus on statistics and numbers but to seek similarities and differences in the accounts of subjective experiences of vocational journeys and to explore how the narrators' decisions to enter, stay, or leave related to their life experiences, ideals, hopes, and emotions. Religious life is embedded in a context where there are power dynamics at play that define authority, gender, class, race, and age differences among other variables, so interactions with established community members were also explored. Through narratives we make sense of our existence, defining who we think we are and explaining our actions and feelings to ourselves and others; thus, it is a process of identity construction (Bruner 1990). The subjectivity of these narratives makes it impossible to take them as objective truths. They describe experiences that are contextualized in time and space and are subject to discourses of power (Smith and Watson 2001). The women who took part in this project did so because they wanted their experience to help others or wanted their opinion heard, so their stories are geared toward these goals. The analysis of the narratives takes into account that individual experiences are always modelled/influenced by their social and cultural context. To understand why women leave or stay in religious life, the story of the communities entered or left by interviewees was included so as to create a dialogue between new members and congregations. No judgment on any of the narratives is offered in the attempt to come to a better understanding of vocational trajectories today. Nevertheless, when put against the data behind the stories and their analysis, and in the response to the Synod (see *Congregation for Institutes of Consecrated Life and Societies of Apostolic Life 2017*) from religious worldwide, a clear pattern emerges of the massive influence of culture, or blindness to the cultural dimension, on the success or failure of attempts by new members to navigate perseverance in religious life.

Narratives of the Call

Is there a future for female religious life in the United Kingdom and Ireland? Has the age and cultural gap between long-term members of communities and those seeking to join them become so great that integration is no longer possible? These were some of the questions that the "Religious Life: Discerning the Future" project took into consideration by interviewing women who had entered or explored religious life in the Catholic and Anglican churches since 2000. Statistics at the time were not encouraging and have not significantly improved. In 2021, a total of fourteen Catholic women entered religious life in England and Wales. This compares with twenty-five in the previous year and shows a significant downward trajectory over the last thirty-four years from the seventy-eight who entered in 1987 (see table 5.1). The interviews with today's generation of explorers of religious life, as well as formators and congregational leaders, enable a collaborative and creative conversation about what might help to build a hopeful future for the religious life of tomorrow.

The UK/Ireland findings were compared at one point with those of the "Study on Recent Vocations to Religious Life"

New Vocations and Vocational Exploration in Britain and Ireland 107

Table 5.1 Entrants into Religious Communities in England and Wales 1987–2021
(Statistics provided by the Conference of Religious and the National Office for Vocation)

Year	Enclosed Nuns	Other Religious Sisters	TOTAL WOMEN	Order Brothers	Order Priests	TOTAL MEN	TOTAL RELIGIOUS
1987	23	55	78	4	56	60	138
1988	12	38	50	1	48	49	99
1989	20	31	51	3	49	52	103
1990	24	30	54	3	49	52	106
1991	14	25	39	1	54	55	94
1992	9	28	37	1	39	40	77
1993	17	17	34	3	45	48	82
1994	12	22	34	1	38	39	73
1995	19	16	35	2	36	38	73
1996	13	13	26	0	32	32	58
1997	10	12	22	3	24	27	49
1998	10	12	22	1	23	24	46
1999	10	12	22	1	20	21	43
2000	10	12	22	1	19	20	42
2001	10	12	22	0	16	16	38
2002	9	10	19	0	15	15	34
2003	12	8	20	2	10	12	32
2004	4	3	7	1	11	12	19
2005	9	4	13	0	18	18	31
2006	6	8	14	2	12	14	28
2007	7	9	16	1	13	14	30
2008	11	15	26	2	12	14	40
2009	9	6	15	0	19	19	34
2010	9	10	19	0	19	19	38
2011	8	17	25	0	19	19	44
2012	11	23	34	0	30	30	64
2013	13	17*	30	0	22	22	52*
2014	18	27	45	0	18	18	63
2015	10	19	29	0	25	25	54
2016	9	22	31	0	29	29	60
2017	9	6	15	0	20	20	35
2018	8	13	21	0	16	16	37
2019	3	16	19	0	24	24	43
2020	5	20	25	0	18	18	43
2021	3	11	14	0	12	12	26

*This figure does not include the 10 former Anglican sisters who established an autonomous monastery within the Personal Ordinariate of Our Lady of Walsingham.

published by the National Religious Vocation Conference (NRVC) in the United States in 2020 (Gautier and Thu 2020). While similar in aims to the UK/Ireland project, there is a significant difference in tone between a report that concentrates entirely on those choosing to remain in religious life and one which includes a sizeable proportion of those who have tried the life and left. In that sense, the aims of the two projects differ significantly, but there is a strong similarity in the positive signs that emerge from both, namely that:

- women continue to hear and respond to the call to religious life;
- they are attracted by the witness of coherent commitment, by prayer and the spiritual life lived in community, by charism, and by whole-hearted mission;
- they are finding strategies to cope with cultural diversity, including intergenerational cultural differences;
- they have a strong commitment to living simply and in solidarity with the poor;
- there is much in both studies that offers hope.

A study entitled "New Measures of Well-Being" identifies several factors essential for creating and maintaining personal well-being (Deiner et al. 2009). These are: meaning and purpose, supportive and rewarding relationships, remaining engaged and interested, contributing to the well-being of others, competency, self-acceptance, optimism, and being respected. Where these elements have been present in the process of vocational discernment and entrance into religious life, respondents have tended to enter a community and remain in it. Narratives of departure from religious life have tended to come from respondents who report that one or more of these elements has been missing to a significant degree.

In the early 1970s, Rosabeth Moss Kanter undertook a study of the long-term continuance or failure of nineteenth-century communes. Kanter's academic method and evaluation techniques have since been subject to academic criticism, but her categories remain useful. She claims that in order to join a community and sustain that commitment, a person needs to detach from some ideas, things, or people, and attach to others. They need to sacrifice some attachments in order to belong to the new community but also to invest in and gain a stake in it. In this understanding, renunciation of some relationships leads to communion with others. The narratives heard within the "Religious Life: Discerning the Future" project are a testimony to how successfully or not such detachments, attachments, investments, renunciations, and communion were mutually negotiated (Kanter 1972:75–125). Interviewees identify the current times as frightening ones in which to attempt religious life because of the declining numbers of sisters and the paucity of vocations, but they continue to see it as a powerful witness to Christ and his Gospel in an increasingly materialistic and selfish world.

What emerges clearly from the narratives is that the guiding story or "myth" that religious life represents is still powerfully attractive to many women of today, the word *myth* being used in the sense of a powerful vehicle for reaching an understanding of a deep truth. Founding figures like Francis and Clare of Assisi and more recent exemplars continue to inspire followers. In this sense, there is no crisis of vocation as such. Women of differing ages and widely varied life experiences are still experiencing the call to join religious communities. The study's overall conclusion is that we are faced with an increasingly urgent crisis of culture. Successful entrance and integration into religious life appears to depend on the "fit" between the individual and the community she enters. Where a new candidate finds herself welcomed and her personal autonomy affirmed, she generally finds the capacity to adapt to a way of life which, even if gladly chosen, presents challenges.

A strong ecclesiology permeates several of the narratives, with the question of numbers and future vocations a concern, but for the sake of the mission of the Church rather than simply the survival of the institution. Participants see themselves as belonging to an historical chain of people who have passed down something precious through the generations, one to the other. Narratives of the call to religious life appear to have changed little over the centuries. Participants describe a strong, all-consuming sense of invitation or even compulsion to respond to an irresistible sense of vocation either present from childhood or coming unexpectedly, as a bolt from the blue. Some inquirers imagine religious life as an adventure, a different and extreme type of life, their images sometimes driven by popular culture and stereotypes of nuns with triggers, such as a Bible passage, a film such as *The Sound of Music* or *The Nun's Story*, or a personal encounter which leads to the realization of a religious vocation. In descriptions of this imagined religious life, there can also be a longing for an idealized way of life, with religious communities featuring as places without conflict where the narrator can find security and a surrogate family, or a community where prayer is at the center. Some interviews show a specific idealization of the monastic contemplative life. Sometimes the seeker herself comes to realize the difference between this idealization and the reality of her own temperament, leading to more realistic and healthy choices of congregation. Whatever the congregation, for some the reality does not match their expectations, with the narratives of leavers showing their expectations as a prelude to the reality they encountered and were subsequently unable to navigate successfully.

If experienced as an interruption to other life plans, this call could prove difficult to accept, but the call can be as persistent as it was challenging or mysterious. In the case of Anglicans, there can be a confusion between the call to religious life and the call to priesthood, which makes discernment all the more complicated. In a vocational journey, there is often a sense of dissatisfaction with life as currently lived and the various options that the secular world appears to offer. There can be a deep sense of a personal love of Christ, sometimes emerging in early childhood but sometimes striking a person forcefully in adult life, either as a development of childhood faith or with the sudden emergence of faith after a life without it. In such cases religious life can seem to offer a radical option for Christ that is powerfully attractive in its all-consuming totality. Narratives similar to those appearing in the study can act as powerful magnets into religious life for inquirers who hear them and who comment on their fascination with others' vocation stories. Sometimes the disillusionment on discovering the reality behind the myth is painful, but the opposite is also true when the reality of religious life turns out to be more positive than originally imagined.

Seeking and Finding

Seventy years ago, Catholic newspapers in Britain were discussing the decline in vocations and the need for strong action to foster new vocations among the young. There is evidence that numbers were already falling in the 1940s and '50s (O'Brien 2017). Energetic efforts were made, and the National Exhibition Centre at Olympia in London hosted several vocations exhibitions (Mangion 2020). Such an outlay of money and energy in pursuit of vocations would be virtually unthinkable today, so opportunities of this kind for finding vocations information are no longer available to contemporary vocational inquirers.

Narrators speak of having little idea of where to turn and of congregations being variable in the level of response they offer to enquiries. Perhaps congregations which have not had an applicant for many years feel a lack of confidence when faced with a vocational explorer, not having formators or a vocations director even though they may not have taken a conscious decision no longer to accept new entrants. For some congregations the use of vocabulary about "vocations strategies" can prove off-putting, suggesting a business-style model alien to the scriptural and historical accounts of a Spirit-led, God-given vocation. Nevertheless, the research indicates that the more coherent and confident a structure of vocational nurturing there is, the more likely a woman is to find the courage to pursue an initial approach. Making first contact is reported as difficult, with inquirers choosing email because they fear rejection, and email is experienced as more impersonal than the telephone or a personal encounter. The role of family and friends features either as a source of support and encouragement or as a discouraging factor in the vocational search, even within believing families. The pride with which some Catholic families formerly received news of a daughter's religious vocation no longer emerges as an expected norm. A key factor in finding a way forward is learning how to pray in a way that might help an inquirer to discern more coherently, though several narratives show that a sense of being called precedes any conscious experience of personal prayer or understanding of God's way within the life of the person being called.

The generosity of congregations in organizing "Come and See" events or workshops on discernment is strongly appreciated by those who have experienced them. In the final instance, "finding the fit" is as much a question of temperament and "family likeness" as anything else. Where congregations or individual religious consulted have felt free enough to understand this, and even to counsel a seeker to look elsewhere if another congregation seems to be the better fit, there have been strong positive outcomes both for the congregation and for the individual concerned.

The quality of discernment by individual respondents and by the congregations or vocations personnel they approach differs widely, ranging from conscious prayer and discernment techniques to using "magical thinking," contacting several congregations and entering the one that answered them first. Others think more systematically, researching questions about a congregation's founder and history, its spirituality, the wearing or not of religious dress, and the congregation's style of prayer and of community life, following recommendations from trusted advisers. For some narrators (particularly in the Anglican responses), the ignorance about religious life was almost total, but despite this they still had a sense of being called to it. Given the ease with which an internet search reveals the existence of the National Office for Vocation, Vocations Ireland, or Compass, the repeated reports of not knowing where to turn are surprising, but this may be because it never occurs to inquirers that such services exist, though there is often strong appreciation when they do stumble across them. If the person sensing a religious vocation has little or no connection with religious, or even with the wider church in terms of priests or other leaders, there can be a sense of being completely at sea with this pressing question. One narrative from Ireland suggests how far the general religious culture has shifted by speaking of religious life as a "taboo" which no one speaks about.

Remarkably, a similar lack of clear processes of discernment on the part of congregations also sometimes emerges. A measure of "survival anxiety" appears to override other considerations, or one inquirer may be seen as a useful companion for another emerging vocation, irrespective of the first inquirer's own individual needs. Narratives suggest that, as an outsider, an inquirer may be considered a useful "buffer" between the community and a struggling sister, or she can feel that she is under pressure to join the community of someone she has contacted when she is merely trying to find out more about religious life in a general sense. Generally, respondents report feeling relief when they finally come to a decision. Discernment inadequately done at the outset has significant consequences for the long-term outcome of an attempt at religious life, with some respondents feeling that they were rushed into deciding because it was convenient for the congregation rather than because it was right for them. Some seekers appear willing to enter a religious congregation with little or no firm understanding either of its charism or its current state, or indeed what religious life even entails. Inquirers may not be informed about essential entry criteria, which later becomes a distressing issue if this prevents them continuing on a path already chosen. This may be because the congregation assumes that these criteria are self-evident, but the lack of basic information on the part of several inquirers, according to their narratives, suggests that clarity is vital at this stage of the discernment process.

There is a cost to a congregation in terms of morale and psychological impact on the established community when someone leaves it, or enters only to find themselves unable to fit in with its norms and expectations. Exploring a religious vocation emerges as a far more isolated and lonely business than in the past, with obvious support structures few and far between. In both the United Kingdom and Ireland, the valuable work of national vocations offices has been crucial in this respect, as has the Compass program in the UK, but narratives also reveal an important role for diocesan clergy here. For some clergy, the only vocation worth fostering appears to be that of the priesthood, and unless the priest in question has some personal connection with religious sisters, there appears to be little understanding of or interest in non-clerical vocations. A similar ignorance or lack of interest appears in Anglican narratives. Conversely, it appears clear that where clergy are well-informed about religious life, they can play a powerful role as nurturers of religious vocations.

Cultural Context

What is different for today's entrants, who are generally older than in past decades, is the cultural context in which the call to religious life is being received. The absence of religious sisters as regular role models in a believer's background dominates many narratives, so for the vast majority the search begins online. The abandonment by many apostolic congregations of monastic styles of dress and living, seen since the Second Vatican Council as inappropriate to their charism and way of life, has rendered sisters invisible to many of those seeking to join them. This perceived invisibility is both at a social level and an ecclesial level, with some women disconcerted when religious do not seem to be a public or visible part of the Church. Even among younger members who have chosen a congregation without external signs, the question of invisibility arises as a challenge. Lack of contact can also lead to an element of fantasy on the part of the seeker who has an idealized notion of religious life which she is not able to test against a known reality. Where sisters are accessible, the age gap can make it difficult to connect naturally. But several narratives speak movingly of the impact that a sister's life can have on others, even when drawing to its end. Loneliness emerges as a repeated factor, whether the loneliness of an emerging faith within a non-faith family and background context or that of seeking help with vocations discernment when knowing no other sisters and approaching clergy or sisters only to be met with a discouraging response. Again, the age and cultural gaps also feature. Sisters remaining active and responsible within ageing and dwindling communities find themselves with increasing workloads, which can affect their availability for vocations promotion both in terms of time and of mental freedom. The relationship with a vocations promoter offering close accompaniment, and the resilience and generosity of a community willing to share their life at depth with someone who may then choose not to join or stay with them, are significant factors in successful contact. In contrast to encounters where inquirers feel pressurized by the survival anxiety of the sisters, an experience of being welcome without expectations leads to a genuine, free, and honest process of discernment. Candidates are quick to pick up elements of freedom or of tension in formation/vocations personnel themselves, whether they are holding the congregation's anxieties about its own future and that of religious life in general, struggling personally with discouragement in the face of falling numbers, or feeling alienated by the attitude of other sisters within their congregation. If explorers feel they are being "sold" religious life, or where there is no sense of vocational discernment being a reciprocal conversation of equals, it can be devastating. But a communicated sense of the worthwhileness of religious life, despite no others joining it, is a strong drawing factor for inquirers who meet it.

Identity

Vocational seekers are trying to understand what pursuing a religious vocation might mean in terms of the life they will find themselves living. Age is not an insuperable barrier, and younger sisters within congregations speak of a strong sense of love and respect for sisters who have lived their consecration with fidelity and zeal over many decades. Seekers see that the identity of religious life is changing and that many of the historical markers, like being in charge of institutional ministries, no longer exist. With this shift some participants perceive a loss of purpose within congregations. Significantly, several interviewees assert the importance of a congregation having a central mission and a strongly defined common ministry. They claim that younger people are drawn to the more well-defined setting of a distinct religious habit and clear rules, as it gives them a sense of confidence in the congregation, but these claims tend to come from those who have opted for congregations where this is the norm. Questions of age and identity do not follow what might be the expected stances taken up by old and young. Some narratives point to a tension between newer members seeking to assert their identity as religious through markers such as distinctive dress and older religious who are strongly opposed to this because of their earlier experience of being stifled by oppressive and alienating rules. All the narratives suggest that religious life is in flux and evolving. There is a need for flexibility beyond the old certainties within established congregations with many older members, as newer members can perceive hanging on to old institutional models as stifling the possibility of new growth and the flourishing of new vocations.

A Question of Age

It appears that a religious vocation is increasingly being experienced by some women as a "second career" move, following a previous major life choice, either within a long-term relationship or a career. They may have experienced a long, low-lying dissatisfaction with their life or a sudden realization that their relationship with God is pivotal for them and that becoming a sister is a viable option for the rest of their life. For some older women this narrows the age gap between newcomers and the established community, but experience has taught some religious leaders and formators to be wary about receiving women at an age where they cannot be expected to change deeply embedded habits and attitudes. If it is challenging for a woman in her late teens or early twenties to adapt to the rhythms and expectations of community life, it can prove virtually impossible for a woman in her forties or fifties, with an already established life pattern, to change it radically.

The issue of age has multiple bearings here. Being the only new sister can render entrants special in a way that can turn oppressive when they have nowhere to hide and can feel under heavy pressure to remain in order to keep the congregation alive. Living among older religious who are open to cultural differences and live their lives with joy and conviction bridges gaps in age and culture and offers strong and attractive role models. Both newer members and their formators comment that age is largely a matter of mentality and attitude, and having a chronological age gap is not necessarily the key issue. Questions around "fit" not only encompass age and culture but also ecclesiology and ideology. A woman who enters religious life is choosing to make a public profession of her faith, ceasing, in some sense, to be a private individual as she becomes a representative of the Church in the perception of many, and this can also present challenges. Where this is not recognized and understood, candidates can find themselves deeply at odds with ideologies alien to their own. The liberalism of generations who emerged during the Second Vatican Council can clash with the need for the John Paul II generation to find greater anchorage in religious certainty. Where the gaps are recognized and efforts made to bridge them, candidates can find that the powerful attraction of the charism, the founder, or discipleship in Jesus Christ himself embodied in older sisters enables them to adapt even to significant and important differences between them and the group that they have joined.

More Questions of Culture

Are religious communities truly open to all? Most congregations would emphatically proclaim their openness to any vocation that God sends them. Their espoused theology of religious life supports this and there would be a conscious rejection of any idea that the class, race, or personal ideology of a candidate might make her unwelcome. But several narratives suggest a gap between the espoused ideologies and those unconsciously operative within the group. This may be based on an unconscious sense of what is normal, so that those who differ from the norm are made to feel it in subtle ways. The Inglehart–Welzel Cultural Map, found in the World Values Survey, shows an increasing global shift in values. From survival values, prioritizing economic and physical security over trust and tolerance, we see countries with greater socioeconomic and political security moving toward self-expression values, each prioritizing environmental protection, tolerance of "the other," and equality and participation in decision-making (Inglehart and Welzel 2010:554; Molina 2017:6). The cohort for this report has generally mirrored this prioritizing of self-expression, tolerance, and participation, while many of them appear to find more of a survival-value mindset within the communities they join.

One of the developments since the mid-twentieth century has been the *embourgeoisement* of religious life. In the early twentieth century there were still large communities of working class Catholics and Anglicans from which religious vocations emerged. Both apostolic and contemplative congregations made a distinction between the sisters who did much of the domestic work and the mothers who sang in choir or taught in the schools. Such distinctions were largely dissolved in the apostolic congregations in the 1950s, but changes in educational and social opportunities also meant the gradual absorption of working class believers into the ranks of the middle class. Poorer workers within British and Irish society today now often come from overseas, but few women from ethnic minorities or lower social and educational status appear to find religious life a viable option. While no religious congregation would be likely to make overt and conscious demands on prospective candidates regarding class-related patterns of behavior, questions arise around how encouraged an inquirer might feel to try her vocation if she sensed herself as an outsider to social patterns of class, race, or ethnicity normative within a given community.

Numerous narratives illustrate seekers' unrealistic expectations that religious and community life will provide the ideal family that has eluded them in their own personal life. There are positive narratives about the experience of leaving challenging family and societal dynamics and entering a way of life where the notion of community is at the heart of the endeavor. But inevitably there is a sense of disillusionment and disappointment when entrants find the dynamics within a community all too normally human. Sometimes, it is not a question of cultural assumptions but simply of the differing needs of a largely retired community and a working member which have not have been noted or provided for. The question of community dynamics and the kind of intimacy considered appropriate in a religious community also comes up. This sense of loneliness and isolation can derive from the sense among formators that novitiate is a "desert period" where solitude is a key factor in enabling the necessary process of personal and spiritual growth and adaption. But the situation of lone novices today is markedly different from the dynamics within which many current formators began religious life and may require a different approach.

These gaps between ideals and aspirations and the lived reality of religious life inevitably attract much comment. Some communities are too stretched in their capacity to deal adequately with new members, and their rhetoric, embedded in their own aspirations and espoused theology of religious life and community, does not match their lived reality. The increasingly transnational nature of religious life also poses particular challenges. The majority of women interviewed were either from the United Kingdom and Ireland (75 percent) or from other Western countries (15 percent). Only six interviewees came from the global South (10 percent). Struggles occur in adapting to Western culture, but this also happens in reverse when women enter an international congregation and are sent to another continent during novitiate where deep ideological gaps emerge. Again, there can be questions of inverse hierarchy based on age, in cultures where respect is predicated on seniority. Where the formator is younger than the novice, this can be particularly difficult. Narratives suggest the need to separate ethnic culture from congregational culture, leaving room for different approaches.

Fitting In

The researchers were struck by the role played by culture in the capacity of new members to adapt and acclimatize within a given community and within the new identity that they take on as religious. Non-European entrants speak of struggling with perceived class prejudice, colonial attitudes, British "aloofness" or unconscious "tribalism" or cliquishness of a given locality or group—even a "group within a group," such as "north" versus "south," alumnae of a congregation's schools or other sponsored works versus "outsiders," and other similar examples. If a community takes as spiritually or behaviorally normative what in fact derives from its majority ethnic culture, a novice from another culture can feel patronized and gain a sense that Western culture is believed to be superior to her own. Moderations required to basic personal habits can reduce candidates to childhood status and leave them feeling belittled. For those experiencing their novitiate overseas in an international or transnational congregation, language limitations can have a profound impact even on such essential areas as novice instruction. A lack of peers can make novitiate an isolating experience, although being in formation with a peer with whom a new entrant has little in common can be just as challenging, with inter- or intra-congregational formation programs becoming a lifeline, despite problems in terms of language and culture.

The theme of feeling disempowered and reduced to childhood during initial formation recurs repeatedly. Older women feel this when their experience is disregarded in favor of a concept of hierarchy, or when a sense is conveyed of there being only one correct way of approaching religious life. Genuine relationships of friendship between generations can flourish, if permitted, and this facilitates living in communities where the age gap is wide, with new sisters feeling reassured and encouraged by the open sharing of the experiences of their elders when it is freely offered, seeing them as custodians of their tradition. Respondents reflect that a person's outlook and mentality are more important for companionship and good cross-generational communication than chronological age. If there is an openness to exchange as equals, without a sense of age-related hierarchy, differences can prove to be a source of enrichment.

Questions of Training and Identity

When adequately trained personnel are low in number, and novices few and far between, offering in-depth formation in religious life can be challenging. Where previous traditional "one-size-fits-all" systems of novitiate formation were often experienced as rigid, some narratives from both current and former members point to a notable void in formation programs. New members report being left to fend for themselves, feeling inadequate to make judgments about the formation program's content themselves if such decisions are left to them, with few clear indications of what is required of them or how they are to absorb the essentials of the life without a clear plan of study or meaningful ministry. Any loss of a clear sense of purpose within the congregation is quickly picked up by new entrants, as is formation content that presents little challenge, which proves particularly frustrating for older women coming from a professional background. Having struggled so much to get themselves to the novitiate in the first place, they appreciate a formation program which feels appropriately challenging. Younger interviewees show a strong appreciation of the clear structures and expectations which go with monastic life or with more traditional approaches, while congregations willing to cater to the different needs of today's new entrants tend to retain them.

A dominant part of the narrative within many congregations is about the necessity of shedding the old self and taking on a new identity, with connotations of starting afresh, healing, and a different way of constructing society in a deliberate rejection of today's secular culture. When a person gives up the standard markers of adult, autonomous life such as their own home and freedom of movement and of determining their finances, work, lifestyle, and relationships, they will inevitably feel a strong initial sense of disorientation and dislocation. While entrants generally understand this in the abstract, in practice many speak of hidden hierarchies which foster feelings of infantilization within religious life, both for newer and established members. Some narrators find instruction that fosters stillness and recollection helpful, but for others the idea that a woman in her forties must be taught how to wash a mug, hold a fork, or sweep a floor because only one way is considered correct or acceptable engenders feelings of dehumanization and disempowerment. New entrants flourish when their talents and gifts are considered, when they are included in decision-making, and when differences are integrated or put aside for the benefit of the whole community. They exhibit pride in their congregation's history and ministries, as well as their current members, and value its capacity to hold together differing theologies and faith perspectives.

Hidden or unconscious hierarchies concerning age, ethnicity, class, and culture, or concealed decision-making and power dynamics embedded within a community are seen as contrasting with inclusion processes in the secular world of work or of other institutions. This can be bewildering and painful and prevent a sense of belonging, especially if acceptance and integration into the community are understood to be conditional, so that the new member has in some sense to "earn" the full acceptance of the congregation that she has joined. New entrants understand that when they join a community as novices, they cannot expect to make decisions about things about which they have had no previous knowledge. But given the age profile and life experience of many of the respondents, some element of participation might be hoped for, and where congregations welcome this, it helps with their sense of integration and of having "come home."

The question of autonomy and power plays a major part in the decision to leave religious life. It is particularly challenging for those who have previously been in abusive relationships of power to have decisions made without consultation or explanation, depending on the mood of those in authority. Interviews reveal a pattern whereby new entrants identify obedience as being principally about listening to God rather than the congregation. More mature entrants may be able to accept decisions which they consider questionable, but they want explanations, and this can prove problematic in groups with underlying hierarchies. The figure of the novice director is key in this. All the narratives that mention this relationship do so in strong terms, whether positive or negative. She may become a mother (or stepmother) figure and adopts or has projected onto her many of their typical qualities. Narrators comment on the levels of control they encounter in the novice director, her level of experience and on the extent to which she has or has not changed with the times. In extreme cases the influence of the novice director is cited as the reason why a sister leaves religious life, or leaves feeling broken. The question of power in relation to the novice can engender deep feelings of conflict or alienation, whether the novice is older or younger than the formator. Interviewees comment on levels of insecurity which they detect beneath dominating exteriors, and on being infantilized by formators unable to cope with being questioned or challenged, so that the novice in doubt about her vocation is left unable to articulate these doubts when it matters. A wide age gap can be problematic, but it can equally present different challenges when novice and director are contemporaries, especially if there is a level of ambiguity on the part of the formator toward her role. A repeated theme in the narratives about formation is that of older sisters relying on patterns from the past which no longer serve well for the current time.

Among congregational leaders and formators there can be conflicting opinions about whether new entrants should simply integrate into an established community or whether the formation community should be tailor-made to their needs. Some narratives speak of novices finding themselves at sea without structured programs, being unsure of what is expected of them, while others express a sense of being under constant observation. In some respects, community life represents both the greatest challenge within a religious vocation, and considerable potential for human and spiritual growth amid the inevitable irritations. The skills to negotiate relationships and work out conflicts with other community members through open communication are recognized as vital. The question of living with those one has not positively chosen comes up repeatedly in descriptions of community life, and narrators comment on the uncertainty that this brings, but also see that the community is both an interior and an exterior space in which God is to be found. Long-term religious frequently comment that community life represents simultaneously one of religious life's primary ideals and primary challenges. Those interviewed speak of their appreciation of shared joy, fun, and support. United by the same goals of prayer, community living, and ministry, they can experience a deep connection with other sisters even where there are no obvious points of cultural convergence. Clashes of personality or of culture exist, especially where unconscious mechanisms of control flourish or close relationships are not encouraged, but where community proves to be the context for genuine personal and spiritual growth into maturity, religious vocations flourish.

Leaving

Both current and former sisters within the study were often at pains to put a positive or ironically humorous construction on their recollections. Even when discussing deeply painful aspects of their experience, they manifested a desire to protect their congregations from criticism, offering their own rationalization of why such pain occurred. Nevertheless, the majority of leavers' narratives display a sense of lasting sadness and, in some cases, of deep trauma. The vocabulary of breaking or being broken appears in some narratives, whether those of entrants or formators, as an expected part of the process of becoming a new person in Christ. Life may present any adult with experiences that engender a sense of brokenness, but some narratives suggest an implicit intent, within a congregation or on the part of a formator, of "breaking" a person as part of the ascetical theology of religious life. In this case there appears a disconnect between the espoused, conscious theology of the group, which is positive and holistic in its self-expression, and the theology which new entrants find actually operating within it, predicated on the need to mold them to a predetermined pattern at whatever cost, even to the extent of experienced abuse.

Some entrants take years to discern the difference between going through a traumatic phase in a challenging vocation and realizing that this is not the life for them. When this happens while the individual still feels called to a life of personal dedication it can prove deeply bewildering but also liberating. A woman wavering in her vocation may try to make herself stay for a variety of reasons, including that of not wishing to disappoint members of the receiving congregation, and the trigger for deciding to leave may come quite unexpectedly. The decision to leave religious life is never taken lightly, but where there has been a well-supported departure, former members are deeply grateful, while being asked to leave can feel like a traumatic rejection, including rejection by God. Most narratives of departure say that the decision to leave religious life felt like a bereavement and was harder than that of joining. Respondents report feeling grateful for being given time to come to terms with this decision, thankful that they are not pushed out of the community before they have processed what their departure means and relieved when they have finally made the decision. Among the reasons for departure listed by respondents are:

- having entered when the individual was not ready fully to adapt to the life
- feeling that religious life was not where she could find her true vocation and identity
- a lack of connection with the group overall
- feeling like a child, stripped of power and not listened to
- problems of depression and mental health
- realizing that the community will not change and that it would be unfair to ask this of them
- discovering a "vocation within a vocation" or falling in love

Where there has been personal, psychological, or financial support for a departing sister there has been immense gratitude. Where no such support has been offered, or assumptions are made that she will be able to manage when in practical terms this is not the case, departing members have expressed a sense of fear and panic. Sometimes leavers have not asked for help, feeling they do not deserve it or have no wish to continue being dependent on the community. Interviews report sadness on the part of the rest of the community, with older members expressing a desire that the departing sister would stay. This can provide a comforting sense of having been loved and wanted but can also add the burden of guilt to an already difficult decision. Most former members interviewed have kept in touch with their congregation and still feel connected to them, looking back on their time within religious life as helping their self-awareness, shaping them, and making them who they are. They miss the shared life, the prayer, and the other sisters, seeing their time in religious life as having added to the quality of their life even if they left with more questions than they began with.

A number of congregational leaders and formators raise the issue of weak catechesis in relation to the challenge of accepting new members today. This is echoed in comments of former members about their current membership of the Church. Some see themselves as living their faith shallowly or only occasionally and yearn for the common prayer which anchored them in a relationship with God. For others their central spirituality has changed. God is not necessarily experienced within the Church, so they have ceased regular formal worship, seeing that a personal spirituality requires neither religious life nor vows.

Moving On

The researchers found the project respondents to be deeply self-reflective women. The immediate years after departure can feel deeply disorientating for a former sister, feeling that she no longer fits anywhere. Some search for another type of community, possibly outside the Church, while others join the single consecrated life. Leaving can feel like losing one's identity, especially when losing the habit or other strong external signs of belonging. Former sisters may carry an abiding sense of loss, shame, and regret, their sense of not being accepted for who they are at the outset, or of not "fitting the mold," leaving them with a deep sense of rejection. Some congregations have anticipated this with considerable compassion and generosity, investing time and financial resources to ensure that a former sister has had every opportunity to process her experience, while elsewhere exiting sisters have been left with a sense of being cut off from their family and their deepest religious identity. While the notion of the "spoiled nun" has thankfully disappeared in general Catholic culture, women leaving religious life speak of a sense of relief, but also of failure and guilt on departure. For some, leaving carries heavy consequences in terms of mental and spiritual health, with narrators stressing their appreciation for the generosity and support of congregations on exiting, while others indicate a limited congregational understanding of the cost of departure to the individual. On the other hand, there are very few indications from the project's entrant cohort that they have any awareness or appreciation of the sense of rejection or abandonment involved in professed members investing emotionally in a new entrant only to see her subsequently leave. On both sides, departure is a painful business.

Mental Health

Both the World Health Organization and the British National Health Service speak of one in four people in the population experiencing mental health difficulties, and this will arise with the same frequency within religious congregations as it does elsewhere. Expectations of religious life as a refuge from problems and issues that exist in secular life can only be disappointed. Where problems are not recognized and addressed—especially in a small, enclosed community—it can have a major impact on all community members. Leavers cite mental health issues of their own or of other community members as a contributing factor to their departure, with communities appearing not to deal proactively with significant cases of anxiety, depression, and psychosomatic illness, leaving novices to attempt the formation process while clinically unwell. This begs the question about the existence or effectiveness of prior psychological screening of applicants, which appears not to be universal, with manifestations of incipient mental illness not always being picked up effectively prior to entrance into the novitiate. Established and new members speak of perceiving a greater psychological fragility in today's generation. Historically, large communities of religious were able to carry members who were frail in their physical or mental health. With communities now generally being older and more fragile, such members can prove harder to absorb and support than in earlier generations.

A View from the Bridge: Experience of Leaders, Formators, and Vocations Personnel

Receiving a new entrant into a congregation is not a neutral experience for those in charge of religious communities or working in vocations promotion or formation of new members. There is adaptation on both sides, as the new entrant explores and discovers both the conscious and the unconscious cultures into which she has entered. At the same time, the established community finds itself having to adapt to her cultural expectations and possibly her very different social, political, and theological understandings of what Christian discipleship means today. Unconscious congregational expectations may be based on a deep collective memory of earlier patterns of formation and on ingrained habits of thought and behavior whose implications are no longer obvious to those for whom they are not the norm.

Religious leaders, formation, and vocation personnel reflect considerable resilience in the face of multiple disappointments as new sisters have come and gone. For any congregation to open itself to new life, long-established sisters need to be open to challenge and the possibility of adaptation and change. It requires intense energy and self-giving for a small or diminished community to welcome someone different into the group, going beyond surface politeness and the friendliness of strangers. It can produce trauma in the established community when a welcomed and cherished new member subsequently leaves. It is a sign of the health of religious life in both Britain and Ireland that so many congregations continue to look to the future with open doors and generous hearts.

Extensive resources have been made available at national levels and that of individual congregations to help today's women in their vocational search, though it remains a challenge to get the right information to the right people. In Ireland, formerly considered a "Catholic country" where the prevailing culture was deeply embedded in the majority Catholic faith, it is no longer possible to assume that young people have any effective connection with the Church or with religious at all. Group activities (such as Samuel Groups, which support vocational seekers) offer help with discernment and spiritual direction for young adults, but group activities requiring regular commitment are no longer working well with a generation used to making decisions about how to spend their time on the spur of the moment. Informing clergy and congregational members about resources and engaging their energies positively also proves challenging, with a level of apathy, fear, or negative thinking among older religious in the face of vocational decline being intuited by inquirers. Several narratives comment appreciatively on congregations which, having decided that new vocations can no longer be accepted, put resources and energy at the disposal of women seeking a new kind of life commitment around the model of religious life. This might be commendable for other congregations where the energy to promote vocations within their own ranks is no longer forthcoming. Successful vocations promotion requires every member of an established community to be exposed to the questions and issues raised in this study and to assume their responsibility for nurturing future religious vocations. Confusion about or disconnection from the whole question of new membership communicates itself to seekers. Awareness of generational cultures features in a recent major study of new entrants in the United States: "Generations are also subcultures, each with its own distinctive preoccupations, memories, and expectations that will render a given religious institute more or less attractive to that generation. The appeal of membership in a given institute will wax and wane as the desires and preoccupations of succeeding generations of Catholics change" (Johnson et al. 2014:80). If there is poor intergenerational dialogue it can crush a vocation, but there is also strong evidence that, with a willingness on both sides to bridge the gaps, age and cultural differences do not inevitably play a negative role for younger religious.

Religious leaders, formation, and vocation personnel speak of difficulties in dealing with new entrants, identified as inflexible and unwilling to adapt to a community setting not tailor-made to suit their personal preferences. Research which looks at members of "Generation Me," born in the 1980s and 1990s and brought up to consider themselves unique and special, with all their dreams reachable, shows how this contrasts with preceding generations whose instincts would still be toward a level of social conformity and prioritizing of the needs of wider society (Twenge 2014). "Fitting in" is no longer a major value for Generation Me, which treasures "I did it my way" above all. However we consider these generational shifts, they must be taken into account when looking at the question of successful promotion and retention of future vocations. There is often a perception that it is the more structured and traditional congregations that are currently attracting new vocations. Research-based studies tell a more nuanced story, with choices differing from one generation to another, but the question of identity and seeking strong community emerges across the varied narratives cited here and impacts not only approaches to vocations promotion but also how the future for religious life is envisaged.

Expert Reflections

The Religious Life Vitality Project, funded by the Conrad N. Hilton Foundation, was researched in 2015 by some members of the same team that produced the project presently under discussion (Sexton and Simmonds 2015). This earlier project drew on the resources of a group of ecumenical theologians, historians, and social scientists with expert knowledge of religious life to reflect on the research data emerging from it. A similar group (named here as reflectors) considered the current research data in a collaborative endeavor, offering fresh responses to it and confirming or challenging the patterns seen as emerging. Whatever the cause of attraction to religious life, they saw that the archetypal myth of the long journey toward life engagement with the *mysterium tremendum et fascinans* has by no means died and is being lived out today in the stories constituting the project data. They compared and contrasted the hopes and expectations of new entrants with the reality that they found, especially when hopes and disappointments appear to be based on cultural and intergenerational norms and expectations, noting the Millennials' and younger generations' lack of experience of community and consequent longing as attested in some recent literature on religious life (see Gilbert 2012; Schneiders 2001).

Reflectors noted that issues of visibility are highly contentious among religious themselves, with the desire for greater visibility carrying an ideological significance, put down to "young people needing structure" or "young people being conservative." But they also note that project transcripts do not suggest an understanding of the habit as connoting a higher status within the Church, just a distinctive one. In light of this, established religious may need to reflect on the extent to which perceptions of religious dress have shifted over the course of the last fifty years. Decreased visibility can lead to misconceptions about apostolic religious life, revealing a possible need for clearer articulation and revitalization of its essential elements of prayer, community, and apostolate. Since candidates may have had little education in catechesis, faith formation, the life of prayer, or moral and ethical theology, the question arises of how religious consecration, the life of the vows, and authority within religious life might be understood and conveyed. Reflectors also questioned what appear to be inadequate initial processes of discernment on the side of both inquirers and congregations, especially where congregations tend to be overeager to have new entrants, despite so much discussion and training about selection and processes in the literature related to religious life of the 1980s and 1990s. They also highlighted the importance of dealing with a potential entrant in a way that makes sense to her, not just within the rationale of the congregation's processes and procedures.

The reflection group perceived a tension within the narratives between the need for person-centered formation, especially with older entrants and lone novices, and the need for clear structures as a framework in which the complex work of building an identity for oneself as a religious can take place. Given the rarity of religious vocations today, a delicate balance is required between flexibility and structure. A major challenge lies in formation processes suited to school-leavers when applied to autonomous adults from professional backgrounds, whose previous history will often lead them to expect basic structures and processes to be in place, to be reasonably clear and not constructed *ad hoc*. Absence of these has an adverse effect on entrants' trust in the congregation, and commitment to the formation process. This need for structure also includes a clear trajectory in life after vows, especially within congregations that are no longer involved at a corporate level in their perceived "traditional" ministry. New members may be drawn to a congregation's spirituality and vision of ministry (or historic ministry), but with few members in active ministry they may be unable to envisage the future in which they will live religious life in practice.

For Rosabeth Moss Kanter, sacrifice (giving up things to belong to a community) goes hand-in-hand with investment (gaining a stake in a community). Both have to be achieved for a successful integration in the new context. In the same way, renunciation (giving up competing relationships) goes with communion (establishing meaningful contact with the community). Sacrifice, investment, renunciation, and communion will only make sense when effectively placed in the reality of today's context. Formators' suspicions over contemporary relationships and modern communications (mobile phones, social media, etc.) may reflect a congregation's belief that detachment is the main demand of a novice, since only once accomplished can "attachment" begin. This can amplify the pressure on novices to disconnect from their familiar world, which is very different from the world experienced by most professed sisters of the same age. Professed sisters may not fully appreciate the extent of the new entrant's lack of understanding of the older sisters' mindset. The greater the detachment congregations demand from a newcomer, the greater the investment that ought to be made in creating attachment, but this does not seem to be the general pattern within the project narratives. The lack of balance here can make it very hard for a novice to remain. Successful transition to life profession tends to be where a community has made attachment a strong element in formation while being gentle about detaching from the previous way of life. A sense of continuity with new members' previous life is not a distracting attachment but an enhancing factor. This ability to retain some measure of older attachments as well as make new ones within the community appears as a strength in the development of vocations.

All commentators noted the clash of social and cultural attitudes and values when it was present in the narratives, noting how dissonance of social and cultural outlook undermined responders' confidence in those who should have been their role models for religious life. Today's candidates expect to be able to raise questions and discuss issues of faith and belief because they are embarking on this radical new life in which the nature of their own being and of ultimate truths is at stake. Used to questioning and debating with friends and work colleagues, they see such questioning as intrinsic to being a mature, modern person. Because there are missing generations in religious communities, with large numbers in the age group of seventy and above and few if any younger members, a "natural shift" of attitudes, practices, and cultural assumptions may not have taken place gradually over time. This means that independently minded, mature new entrants can be experienced as presenting a challenge to the embedded culture of a community that may have coalesced and rigidified over the years, when in their own judgement they are simply expressing what is normative in their world. Reflectors detected among new entrants a conscious and unconscious communion ecclesiology which they expect to find in religious life and in a Church that finds its ultimate basis in relationships: between people, with God through Christ, and in the Holy Spirit. This contrasts with their perception of a culture within communities experienced as hierarchical and deferential rather than *communio* or having a primarily personalist understanding of relationship and human development. Ultimately, the question here is how a congregational charism might be reborn as a genuine rediscovery and rebirth, while ensuring the "change of life" or "conversion of life" that religious profession implies.

The process of departure from religious life, when well-handled on both sides, can be one of growth and gratitude. Reflectors were concerned at the unresolved pain that remains for a number of narrators, even when prior to novitiate they had been mature women in midlife, with good experiences of changes or challenges in their working lives. The process of departure from religious life was put into the context of secular personnel management, and challenging questions were raised about the poor handling revealed in relation to matters of identity, self-esteem, and future direction. But it was noted that even those who recall a painful departure from religious life remain strongly supportive of the vocation in a general sense.

Summary and Conclusions

Formators and newer and former members are often united in their apprehension about the future. Despite the relatively small number of women entering religious life in Britain and Ireland today, this way of life clearly still retains the power of attraction and remains a viable option for women seeking the radical following of Christ. The attraction that newer members feel to a community life based on more than sharing a living space together can feel threatened by the increasing tendency for religious to live on their own, but the desire for intentional community remains, despite numerical diminishment. Many religious congregations have made heroic efforts to remain open and generous toward women of very different ages and cultures coming forward to try their vocation. The fragility of structures in today's religious life can prove a challenge both to those seeking to enter it and to those seeking to maintain it in a sufficiently healthy way for new entrants to find viable. A more acute appreciation of the culture from which today's applicants are emerging is clearly needed if religious life is to survive and flourish. Different patterns of commitment and belonging are emerging in the new monastic communities, sharing the original charism or a mixture of charisms outside the structure of vowed membership. This is a possible response for the future, deriving from the primordial vocation of baptism rather than from religious consecration.

The figure of Rachel weeping for her lost children is indicative of the fragility of today's religious life, but she is not a figure of tragedy and mourning. Even though she is connected in the Gospels with the loss of children and a future, through the eyes of faith she remains a figure of prophecy and hope for those prepared to rebuild the structures of religious life and re-envisage its culture anew.

6

Women's Religious Life Vocations in Mexico
Elements for Further Reflection

Fr. Luis Fernando Falcó, MSpS

There is a great difference between how consecrated life is lived and how, for the most part, life in secular society is lived. That fact is not something that should come as a surprise, nor does it represent a new phenomenon. It is characteristic for the consecrated way of life to sustain and maintain within itself a structural difference which gives it a specificity and a unique identity (Turcotte 2001a). This is based on the tension raised by the type of paradox found in the Gospel of John: "you are in the world, but you are not of the world" (John 17:11-14). This is an ideal proposal which consecrated life claims as one of its major signs of identity.

This distance should never be dissolved, since it is an essential characteristic of consecrated life. But neither is it in keeping with the desire of consecrated persons to serve as a sign to the world to maintain a state of insoluble strangeness, so that this group of Christians, committed to the Catholic Church, comes to be perceived as representing a socially unrecognizable way of life that goes beyond normal expression. Throughout the long centuries of Christianity and until half a century ago, there existed mechanisms of communication between the one world and the other. The Catholic Church and Latin American societies to some extent shared a horizon of meaning that was rooted within broad layers of the population.

It was possible to recognize a certain common background that existed between the idealized values of traditional Christian and culturally Christian society and what was being sought within consecrated life. However, these mechanisms of communication that had existed in various forms throughout the centuries of Christianity and permeated Latin American societies from their foundation gradually faded into an almost impassable distance after the middle of the twentieth century.

Latin American societies, Mexico among them, have gone through a process of modernization and pluralization of beliefs and lifestyles during the twentieth century, which means that the consecrated way of life is now perceived as socially alien. This structural distancing makes the consecrated life of women probably highly valued "in itself," but it does not make it any less strange, as it is shown in the national survey on religious matters "Creer en *México*" (IMDOSOC 2014). It can be recognized as notably distant from the mainstream of young women typically socialized within cultural parameters, such as those that are being imposed on broad strata of Mexican society.

This gap is expanding without religious women showing in definite ways clear signs of adapting their way of life and how they present this vocational choice in such a way as to open channels of communication which would make it socially plausible that the consecrated lifestyle is a possible life choice for groups of young believers and seekers of meaning.

The way in which this distancing between young women and religious life occurs in Mexico today is a subject that needs to be investigated empirically, to discern how it occurs in concrete terms. There is a further question of what it would imply to overcome this distancing and what it might mean for young women possibly interested in this way of life to enter and adapt to the everyday rhythm of consecrated life, when they have been socialized within the parameters of secular society that lie far distant from the specific way of life of religious communities.

Everything indicates that women's religious life in Latin American countries such as Mexico has still not systematically considered the necessary efforts at adaptation so that the formation programs of its institutes are capable of offering meaningful and vital alternatives, and providing cultural and identity resources, so that young women can identify themselves and eventually fulfill themselves subjectively. It is astonishing that the description below was written sixty years ago and is still valid in many religious life environments within Mexico:

> Religious women often appear as if living in a closed world, withdrawn into themselves, poorly connected with the outside world. A religious congregation quite often produces the effect of a fortress, whose drawbridge can only be lowered stealthily and fearfully. A certain concept of separation from the world leads, they think, to a kind of psychological isolationism. Hence the lack of dialogue with those immediately around it, for lack of common interest and identical wavelength. Even if, before entering the convent, the nun has been immersed in the world thanks to her own environment, and perhaps even thanks to her apostolate, she soon becomes disoriented. She encloses herself in a hermetic enclosure or at least in an enclosure which has no openings other than narrow skylights and not wide bays onto the outside world. . . . On the other hand, the material and psychological distancing from the world leads the

nun to withdraw into herself, into her own community (Cardinal Suenens 1963:29–30).

Although the processes of religious change as they are occurring in Mexico are affecting the horizon of meaning of young Mexican women above all, making them less inclined to listen to a vocational call to religious life, as the *Latinobarómetro* (2020) survey shows (table 6.1), there is a growing gap in the religious self-understanding of young Latin American women which affects the possibility of making a call to the religious life socially viable. Consider the data shown here in the table of religious commitment from the *Latinobarómetro* survey.

Table 6.1 Religious Commitment: How would you describe yourself?

Category	Total	15–25	26–40	41–60	61 and over	N
Very devout	8.8%	7.1%	8.9%	8.9%	10.3%	84
Devout	42.3%	39.9%	38.4%	42.1%	52.4%	405
Not very devout	37.1%	37.2%	39.9%	37.2%	31.2%	356
Not devout at all	11.8%	15.8%	12.7%	11.7%	6.0%	114
N	959	174	296	333	155	959

If we agree that it is usually common and expected that young people with a live and active religious commitment are those who will be more interested in learning about religious life, it is worth paying attention to this measurement made for Latin American countries. These results from the latest *Latinobarómetro* survey, which asked about religious commitment, report that only 7.1 percent of young Mexicans (between fifteen and twenty-five years of age) say they are very devout. When the results are restricted to Catholic respondents of the same age, it is even lower (6.3 percent). The results drop even further when cross-referenced with young people's level of education. This data-based phenomenon is echoed by the notable reduction of vocations to religious congregations in Mexico, as shown by current evidence.

Recent research on elderly sisters in México (Falcó, Hernández, and Leyva 2021) was carried out by the Collaborative International Research Team, in which the Cruces research team on religious life participated, together with the Centre for Research in Religious Life and Apostolate (CERRA) in Nairobi, in partnership with the Center for Applied Research in the Apostolate (CARA) at Georgetown University. The research offers a fairly clear perspective on the meager numbers of younger sisters that characterize female religious life in Mexico today. According to this research, the average age of women in Mexican religious congregations is sixty-two years. Over time, the proportion of sisters who are between thirty and fifty years old is getting smaller. In fact, over a quarter (27 percent) of the religious institutes surveyed in Mexico for this project report that more than half of their members are over fifty years old. Table 6.2 displays the age distribution of women religious in Mexico at this time, as reported by the religious institutes.

Table 6.2 Age Distribution of Members of Institutes of Women Religious in Mexico

Age Category	Number of Sisters	Percentage of all Sisters
<30	1,035	7%
31–40	1,817	12%
41–50	1,625	11%
51–60	2,840	19%
61–70	1,906	13%
71–80	2,869	19%
>80	3,114	20%
Total	**15,206**	**100%**

As for the numbers of vocations entering the institutes, entering vocations are increasingly scarce, too few in number to reverse the declining trend in age that is shown in table 6.2. The picture of entering vocations is grim, as seen from the vantage point of the 161 institutes that responded to the above-mentioned survey on older sisters in Mexico. Table 6.3 shows the total number of aspirants and postulants reported by these institutes. Altogether, the 458 entering vocations represent less than 4 percent of the total membership of these reporting religious institutes. Interestingly, it seems that the smaller institutes (those with less than 100 members) are doing a bit better, proportionally, at attracting new vocations. Aspirants and postulants make up 5 percent of the total numbers reported in small institutes (of less than 100 members) but only 3.3 percent of the total numbers reported in larger institutes (of more than 100 members).

Table 6.3 New Entrants to Institutes of Women Religious in Mexico

Type	Number of New Entrants	As a Percentage of all Members
Aspirant	253	2.1%
Postulant	205	1.7%
Total	**458**	**3.8%**

What part of this collapse of vocations can be attributed to the de-Christianization of the culture and social identity in Mexico, and what part might be due to the lack of adaptation on the part of women's institutes (and men's too, obviously)? This is difficult to clarify and requires qualitative research on specific, empirically well-defined formative spaces. Generally speaking, it can be argued that there is a concurrence of two relatively independent factors that come together to give rise to this growing alienation. However, it is possible to gain certain insights which may shed light on how this growing distance is occurring between what consecrated life offers and the usual cultural modes of young Mexicans, via the experiences of some candidates who have entered houses of formation of religious men and women in recent months or years.

In order to observe the distance between the practices of daily life into which the majority of young Mexicans and Latin Americans have been socialized and the things they face when they arrive in consecrated life, we have asked them to describe, subjectively, the cultural break implied in coming to live in a religious community. It is therefore very thought-provoking to observe how those in formation from more than forty women's and men's institutes, 90 percent of them located in Latin America, recently responded when asked in a reflective exercise with their formators in September 2022: *When you came to live with us or when you met us, what were the practices of life (customs, ways of living, routines) that were most difficult for you to understand and live?*[1]

Those religious who have been living this lifestyle for years, and for whom the very peculiar behaviors and practices within the religious community have become as natural as if they were something obvious or self-evident for the young people who come to their houses of formation, should find the spontaneous responses of these young religious very challenging. The quotes presented here reveal this mismatch; a few snippets should suffice. Here are some of the peculiar behaviors and practices reported by one of the groups:

Eating all together; asking for things I need; the particular greeting Sisters are used to saying; to take the bath in a shower; eat with cutlery; the conversation we must have at the table; adapting to a particular regulation for every activity during the whole day.

---

1. See Cruces, Systematic Formators Course of 2022, IX edition. In the module on the challenges of today's culture to formation for religious life, we began with a very simple research exercise in which formators were invited to ask those in formation, in a direct and unprompted way, what they had found difficult to understand and live when they entered religious community. The quotes presented here are a small part of the responses that tend to show quite a number of similarities.

The early time for waking up, having meals at the same time every day, every activity has a specific hour to be done, the way the sisters dress and the way we have to dress up. I was used to working at night, and I must go to bed early.

Asking for permission on many issues; ask for very personal things.

Waking up so early in the morning, the dress we must wear, talk and laugh quietly.

The way I have to express myself; permissions; all the rules that we have to follow.

Having a daily schedule and all the rules in the community and obedience.

Quitting my cell phone and social networks; not visiting my family and friends frequently.

The routine recreational activities; long time for praying.

The way we eat, the established time for eating, everything depending on community.

Leaving aside personal times and activities; one has to be punctual and prompt in every activity.

The food we eat in here; leaving aside my own interests and hobbies; readings during the meals.

The schedule that cannot be changed and learning obedience.

A lot of words I never heard before in my life: "Make teams with the mates."

Obedience, when it means giving up some practices that were common in my life, like having my own money.

Another group spontaneously expressed their experiences of similar peculiarities:

Tak[ing] the shower with cold water has been such a big challenge.

Waking up early in the morning every day; the responsibilities [for which] I was in charge now.

Few times to share, talk with the sisters, and listen to music as I used to when in my family.

Rivalry amid the sisters in community; They speak about sisterhood and mutual love, and then I got to know that there [are] many sisters who hate each other.

I feel sleepy while in the praying time. The everyday routine, the schedule never changes.

I felt obligated to talk about myself and my feelings to people I don't trust or even know well.

To have a precise hour to do everything in the day; eat with cutlery; that there is a specific routine to wash dishes.

Leave my cell phone; and not calling my parents. One has to say the truth always.

To leave the clothes I used to wear. Keep quiet and not listen to music and no more chats [on] the cell phone.

With this routine I felt tired early in the day.

I used to eat anything I liked, not obligated to eat what they give us.

To think in my own history; recall what happened to me as a child.

Ask permission for most things I want to do.

Get used to staying at the convent most of the time and not going out to some other places; not going out with my friends.

Asking for personal items I need; the clothes we must wear.

In these variegated responses, there is a bit of everything, referring to the very different "orders of the day" which constitute the daily life of those who dare to take on the challenge of religious life and the major cultural rupture involved in coming to try their vocation in a community of consecrated life. Incidentally, the voices represented here are mostly those of women.

From among the spontaneous comments of these young people, the randomly chosen snippets presented here are revealing in that they include so many different issues. They range from the seemingly inconsequential behavior of those who say that "taking a bath in cold water has been quite a challenge," to the importance given to letting go of fundamental relationships including everything that is involved in "not seeing family" or becoming detached from extensions of the self that are so fundamental in technologically mediated societies such as "giving up my mobile phone." Then there are other practices that are complicated for young people who are beginning life in religious communities, such as those that reflect certain habits that have been a feature of religious life for decades or even centuries, like "[keeping] silence, talking or laughing quietly, asking permission, having to ask for things, especially personal things, or the whole ritual of washing dishes," not to mention issues that end up being very relevant because they touch on the image of the person, such as "giving up the clothes I used to wear or getting used to being locked up."

This is how the young women describe the universe of daily life practices of religious women, which are strange to them because they are incomprehensible or indecipherable to them, and because they do not find reference points or similarities in the ways in which they have lived their own socialization processes. It is not so much religious understandings or the truths of faith that are difficult to accept for a young woman who is considering the religious life or searching. It may not be the sense of a life of special consecration, which religious congregations claim to support, that is difficult for young people with some disposition toward the cultural migration involved in coming to live in a community. It is that they do not find a point of reference in the ways of living and developing that populate their living environments. It is not that they are superficial or without religious meaning or that they lack a spiritual quest. Rather, the challenge for this social outsider to immerse herself, in one fell swoop, into the daily life practices of religious communities is that she can feel absurd, strange, or meaningless. The day-to-day practices of consecrated life do not represent anything that gives meaning to the life of a more or less well-socialized young woman.

The problem is that not a few religious communities are so used to living enclosed in their own worlds that they do not realize how certain habits, long-standing customs, and uncritically repeated routines can become an insurmountable barrier that is difficult for religious women who are vocation promoters and formators alike to understand. They accuse young women of spiritual unavailability when it is their approach to formation that is unavailable for adjustment or adaptation and is concerned only with repeating what they received before from their predecessors.

When an institute of religious life experiences a lack of new vocations, as is happening in Mexico today, it is apparently easy for institute leaders to repress any disposition to renew their traditional way of living and instead to place the blame on youngsters and modern culture. In doing so, they avoid taking on a continuous discernment of those routines, mores, and relations that ought to be adjusted to the culture that is changing so fast. As a result, they prefer to silently abstain from offering the gift of religious life to new generations. That should not happen!

7

Vocation to Religious Life
Through the Lens of Young Religious in India

Metti Amirtham, SCC

Introduction

Religious life reflects the endless story of call-and-response amid changing demographics. In India, even though the vast majority of the population belongs to the Hindu religion and Catholics are only 2 percent of the total population, women and men from India continue to respond to the call of God to follow Jesus radically through the religious way of life. Table 7.1 presents some of the religious demographics of the Catholic Church in India (Conference of Religious India 2023).

Table 7.1 Total Numbers of Women and Men Religious in India as of 2021

	Brothers	Priests	Sisters — Apostolic	Sisters — Contemplative	Total
Total Religious Congregations	17	19	282	10	399
Number of Religious Superiors	39	217	706	63	1,025

		Professed	Average Age
Brothers		2,031	48.08
Priests		25,523	43.90
Sisters	Apostolic	102,172	48.40
	Contemplative	884	52.85
Total		130,610	47.70

These consecrated women and men are a tremendous blessing to India and the universal Church. They are willing to go the full length of giving themselves to Christ. They consciously make a radical gift of self for the love of Jesus, the love of the Church, and the love of the world. They are actively involved in various ministries in India and around the globe. They have contributed significantly through their presence, life, and mission. They have played a greater role in the lives of the people through their ministries of education, health care, evangelization, social work, and pastoral activities.

Not only have they provided educational, pastoral, spiritual, and basic human ministries, but the consecration of their lives in imitation of Jesus Christ is profound. In a world that is so consumeristic, overly corrupted, globalized, and so lacking in respect for elders and authority, these men and women have vowed to be poor, chaste, and obedient as Jesus.

However, the current statistics on the status of consecrated religious in India reveal that the number of candidates joining religious life is dwindling fast. The vocation to consecrated life has become an essential concern of every religious congregation in India today. Vocation is a major topic in most of the institutes' leadership meetings. Hence this chapter attempts to look at religious life today through the lens of young religious to identify and strengthen vocations to religious life in India.

Methodology

This chapter presents the consolidated findings from interviews, conducted in October and November 2022, among one hundred religious sisters and brothers working in different parts of central and southern India, aged between twenty-five and forty. Among them, forty-five are at the final stage of their preparation for perpetual vows. A questionnaire was given to them to learn how they experience religious life, their understanding and perceptions about vocation promotion, what sustains and challenges them in their commitment, and what could promote more vocations to religious life in India.

The following questions[1] were given to the young religious men and women to reflect on and voice their concerns:

- How do you experience religious life today?

- What's been your experience? What were you looking for? What did you find? If you entered and stayed, why? Has your religious life changed since you entered? Where? How?

- Are there ways in which religious life in India needs to change?

- How do you see the present status of religious vocation in India?

- What do we need to promote or facilitate more vocations in India?

Summary of the Responses

A summary of the respondents' responses to the questionnaire is presented below.

Experience of Religious Life

The consecrated religious tell us that they experience religious life as a precious gift of God and find meaning and satisfaction in living this life. Nevertheless, they still find religious life challenging and demanding at times. Here are some of the challenges they experience, in their own words.

---

1. These questions were formulated to elicit answers from religious men and women; the participants were chosen randomly.

Some speak of the challenge of complacency:

> We feel more challenged and demanding as we become more comfort seekers, selfish-minded, craving power and position, name and fame.

> Religious cannot take up the cross joyfully but become sad and grumble at even minor pains and difficulties.

Others worry about the appearance that worldly concerns have higher priority than serving the poor:

> We find politics and artificiality in the provinces and [in the] congregation.

> Sometimes we put on masks, and instead of building communities, we spend our whole energy constructing many buildings.

> Congregations are [more concerned with] generating income and money in their apostolate than serving the poor.

> We are called and consecrated to serve the poorest of the poor, but we are attached to our families and relatives and care for their well-being.

Still others write about the challenges of an unequal distribution of power and privilege within their communities. This causes a lack of unity that reflects poorly on the public image of religious life:

> Jobs, opportunities and apostolic ministries are allotted based on caste, friendship, family background and like-mindedness.

> The elders and those in the position[s of authority] are reluctant to teach and equip the young for the future mission.

> The lack of unity and understanding among the sisters in the community scandalizes the public.

Satisfaction or Dissatisfaction?

Since most of the respondents are younger members of religious congregations, they are quite satisfied with their chosen vocation. They express their happiness and satisfaction with religious life in these words:

I am drawn to religious life primarily by a sense of call and a desire for prayer and spiritual growth. Hence, I am happy and satisfied.

Happy to give myself freely and willingly for the needs of others.

Happy to take up challenges and live a witnessing life.

Happy to do God's mission with prayerful support, love, care, concern, and understanding of the sisters.

Some religious are delighted because they live their lives with total commitment and dedication. All the same, some religious are happy because their happiness relies on power, position and needs, which are fulfilled completely, and they lack nothing but receive everything in abundance in the congregation.

Some members find that some are influential role models of fidelity, courage, and audacious hope.

A few of these newer members express frustration and dissatisfaction with religious life. Not everything has happened as they expected, and they share some of the disappointments they have experienced:

Because education (that they desire), power, and authority are not given to them as per their expectations, and their ambitions are not met.

Groupism, casteism, individualism [by] comparison, non-recognition and the politics involved in our congregations make the religious sad.

> *Sometimes, religious people seem to be unwilling to face the challenges of this way of life and are not ready to accept the corrections of the formators.*

Status of Religious Vocation in India

These younger religious have many opinions about the current state of religious vocation in India. Some are concerned that religious vocations appear to be declining, following a pattern noted in other parts of the world. They are also concerned that those who present themselves with a vocation may not have the right motivation or depth of faith necessary to prevail in religious life:

> *The present status of vocation is rapidly decreasing, and sometimes we find that the vocations to religious life are not authentic but very shallow.*

> *Sometimes, it is visible that the vocations are primarily from economically poor families; some join the religious life to equip themselves to become skillful [enough] to get a job.*

Others offer a more optimistic take on the status of religious vocation, noting that new vocations continue to come forward, sometimes from unexpected sources:

> *India is able to get vocations from tribal belts. That's a sign of hope.*

> *Sometimes, religious search for vocations from their areas or [from the] areas of their castes, natives, and languages.*

Reasons for the Loss of Vocation

Although vocations to religious life are found in some areas of India, there are no vocations in some parts. There are many reasons for this, and these newer members of religious congregations share their opinions about why this may occur. Some feel that the decline in vocations may be due to changes in the style of family life:

> *Many families have few children; Often, it is one [child] nowadays.*
>
> *Fewer children in families and growing job opportunities for women.*
>
> *Lack of support from family and friends: families are not encourag[ing vocations]. The social environment in the family today is not favourable; the situation with family and friends is not very different. Family support is no longer guaranteed; often, the most significant opposition comes from their families—even those who consider themselves Christian—there is emotional blackmail and exaggerated extortion to put them to shame. They refuse to support their choice or even question it: "But what are you going to do as a religious? You can do much more here without constraints or changing your workplace."*

Some newer religious see changes in Indian culture and values as eroding vocations to religious life. They point to issues such as a rise in casteism in religious life, changing societal values fueled by mass media and technology, and the effects of these changes on family life:

> *Casteism has crept into religious life: The families are afraid that their sons or daughters will suffer due to casteism, fear of being sent out later. This might bring stigma to the family. This might affect the dignity and prestige of the family.*
>
> *India is witnessing a profound change of values eroding the moral and natural principles. India is in a fundamental shift in epochs giving birth to the emergence of a new humanism governed by a new culture and value system, which*

are increasingly controlled by media and technology. The influence of the compelling means of social communication and the popularization of technology has deeply impacted the lives of Catholic families and, in particular, the youth. Misguided by media, youth often fall prey to the temptations of false havens, to the culture of fun and entertainment, filled with passion and without the strength to love. The present generation lives in a culture of fragmentation where stable values and permanency have no meaning.

The influence of mass media among the youth and the faith formation of the children and youth in the family should be taken care of properly.

Others see the decline in vocations as stemming from the religious congregations themselves. They feel that their congregations are out of touch with young people and that the "Come and See" experiences that are provided are not attractive to young people. They recognize that they do not have the time to cultivate personal relationships with the young because of their institutional responsibilities. In general, they feel that religious do not live a witnessing life to the life chosen, and they fail to be role models for their vocation:

The congregations are worried about vocation and want young people. But the reality discloses that they need more time to be ready to understand the young. Instead, they want to impose on them what they have.

"Come and See" experiences are not often attractive to youth.

Lack of house visits because we are buried in the institutions and our responsibilities within the community.

Youth search for models, and the religious need to live a witnessing life.

Lack of exemplary and witnessing life of the religious.

Finally, these newer members lay some blame for declining vocations on the formation provided for those entering religious life. They recognize that these problems come from both directions—on the part of the candidates as well as from the formative community:

> *Expectations for the candidates (i.e., restriction to use mobile) from the congregations are high, and they are also harshly treated during the formation, even for minor issues/ mistakes.*
>
> *Today's youth are unprepared and unwilling to face the challenges in the community and ministries.*
>
> *The formation program could be more enjoyable. The formators often expect them [candidates] to be like them [vowed religious] and [do] not accept them as they are. The young must be accepted as they are in the state where they are found and helped to achieve the highest goals. Young people have a sense of life or are seeking it. If it is true that many young people, for different reasons and circumstances, tend to reduce life to the simple biological cycle of birth, growth, reproduction, and death. In that case, it is also true that many young people discover life as a vocation, a mission, and a 'dream' and so strive to make it a reality.*
>
> *Some English-speaking congregations send away their candidates, even when they do not know how to speak English in the first year.*

Concrete Suggestions for the Betterment of Religious Life

We asked these newer members of religious congregations to tell us some ways that religious life in India needs to change to improve the experience for those entering religious life and those who will be its future. They had many suggestions for improvement, often resonating with the themes of communion, participation, and mission from the recent documents collected from around the world in advance of the Synod on Synodality. Some said that religious need to revisit their congregation's charism and try harder to live it out. They feel that a change in attitude and orientation will help those called to a religious vocation feel welcomed and respected throughout their formation:

> *We must return to our congregation's origin and strive to live that spirit.*
>
> *Avoid criticism over the mistakes made by the sisters and give them another chance to lead a better religious life.*
>
> *Sisters should not be abused verbally and emotionally within the community and congregation.*
>
> *Every sister has the responsibility to maintain religious decorum.*
>
> *The sisters must be consulted before sending them for studies and new ministries.*

Others suggest that there are many ways that religious formation can be improved. They consider it unhelpful that some ministries are labelled as menial and that juniors usually are placed in these menial ministries, often for years. They feel that members in formation should be given more opportunities and should not be punished when they express their opinions and feelings:

> *The religious should not segregate and label the ministries as menial and higher.*
>
> *Juniors must be sent for studies after two years of community living instead of placing them for kitchen work for three to four years.*

> *Juniors must not only be used for work, especially the manual work of the community, and assist the authorities in doing their personal work like washing their clothes, ironing, and so on.*
>
> *Opportunities must be provided for the younger ones and accompany them as they execute the given responsibility.*
>
> *Revengeful report writing should not be done about juniors when they express their opinions and feelings.*

Newer members also have many suggestions for leaders and for more helpful ways that leadership could be exercised to improve the experience for all in religious life:

> *Authorities must be trustworthy and not impose their likes and mindsets on others, especially newcomers.*
>
> *Authorities should consider all the members equally and not treat them differently based on their caste and language.*
>
> *Should not focus on the caste and background of the sisters, especially the newly professed.*
>
> *Look for leaders to lead the congregations at the time of the election, not based on one's caste.*
>
> *Do away with those leaders who form groups based on caste.*
>
> *A few authorities in the congregation remain as perpetual superiors, principals and headmistresses in different places; instead, they must be given the change of office and other responsibilities too.*

Finally, these newer members have many suggestions for ways that religious could improve themselves to better align their vocation with the signs of the times. These improvements could help religious life to be more attractive to those who are considering a vocation as well as more effective for those who are living out their vocation:

The religious need to update their ministries and themselves according to the signs of the times and respond to them promptly.

Religious should be updated with political and social knowledge.

Religious should participate in public functions and awareness programs and give valuable suggestions and opinions.

The religious need to leave their comfort zone and reach out to the unreached.

Genuine love, forgiveness, and acceptance must be built among the religious instead of being led by groups, favoritism, egoism, and gossip.

Needs of the Hour

These younger members of religious congregations have many opinions and suggestions for promoting religious vocation among the youth in India. They suggest several ways to approach the youth in parishes and introduce them to religious life:

Let us move to the interior villages, visit them and find out the interested boys and girls.

A handout about the importance of religious life could be distributed to the youth.

We should provide space for the youth to get involved in the parish's activities.

[We could] arrange a program for youth to dance, sing, play, and exhibit their talents and skills.

After the Mass, we can gather the youth, conduct games and activities, and play with them to build a relationship with them.

During catechism and youth meetings, we can give current news about the church and its need for religious in the church.

They also suggest ways that the newer tools of social media can be used to promote vocation among youth:

More religious must be in charge of the youth group and youth animation and create a WhatsApp group and inspire them by sending short films, memes, videos and boosting messages for the day.

Conducting the vocation camp creatively by using mass media and uploading the ministries of our congregation on YouTube.

Another way these newer religious think that vocations could be promoted is through the institutions in which the religious are ministering. There are many ways for religious to highlight and promote their vocation in their ministries:

Observance of Vocation Awareness Week could be organized in the diocese or the institutions (i.e., schools, colleges, parishes, and hospitals).

Give more importance to the Christian children in our institutions and play saints movies in the schools during catechism classes.

Visiting the children and students' families of our institutions is a must.

Each religious should take up the responsibility to promote vocation, especially when they go for home holidays, during travelling, visit the girls, and keep constant contact with them.

Vocation promotion begins with the office of vocations, but it does not end there. These newer religious have many ideas to strengthen the office of vocations and extend vocation promotion through all levels of religious life. They note that vocations also need to be nurtured among those already in religious life through strong and ongoing formation programs:

Appoint not only vocation promoters in the province but also in the community. There needs to be more than an appointment. They must make consistent efforts.

There should be a separate annual budget prepared for vocation promotion.

Vocation promotion information on the congregation's website or a distinct website could be thought of.

The best way to promote vocation is to nurture the vocation of members who already live in the congregation through life-long formation programs and to ensure that a solid formation experience strengthens it.

One of the most important ways religious institutes could support newer members in their vocation is through listening and dialogue along the journey.

These newer religious also recognize that vocation promotion activities of the Church worldwide can be powerful tools to promote vocation. They also suggest ways parishes and other institutions can use these tools to encourage vocation locally:

World Day of Consecrated Life (Feb. 2nd) should be celebrated in parishes and institutions.

The "Good Shepherd Sunday" invites the Church to pray for and promote vocations in all their forms publicly. Many parishes and religious institutes commemorate this day with a prayer for vocations and vocation promotion events.

Conclusion

The ministry of vocation facilitation is a shared responsibility of religious leadership, vocation promoters, and vowed members. Hence, all must get involved in vocation facilitation in India. The younger, newer members of religious congregations interviewed for this project are filled with creative ideas for promoting vocations. They also share openly the joys and the challenges they experience in religious life. They echo many of the same joys and challenges voiced by other young religious in other parts of the world, as heard in the other chapters of this book. They are committed to living their vocation joyfully and fully. Their wisdom deserves to be heard. As long as the charism of religious life remains attractive and necessary, young people will respond to religious life, and there will always be vocations.

8

Experiences of Newer Religious Vocations in Kenya

Bibiana Ngundo, LSOSF

Introduction

Religious life in Kenya is still a relatively attractive option among young people. In spite of the looming threat of decline in vocations to religious life, congregations in Kenya are still receiving newer entrants every year. Among those who discern a vocation to religious life, the majority tend to enter a religious institute upon completing high school. In 2017 and early 2018, we distributed a survey designed to collect data from new entrants to religious life to all identified houses of formation in Kenya. These formators shared the survey with 500 individual aspirants, candidates, and postulants in their congregations. Of these 500 identified women and men, a total of 407 responded to the survey, which represents a response rate of 81 percent of the entrance class of 2017 in Kenya.

We gathered information about the characteristics and experiences of these men and women, using a similar questionnaire and methodology to that used for "The Entrance Class of 2016" survey, which the Center for Applied Research in the Apostolate (CARA) conducted among U.S. religious institutes. The report relies entirely on quantitative and qualitative responses that were contained in the survey.

This essay summarizes a portion of the responses to the survey, with a specific focus on the background of newer religious, their attraction to religious life, and their experience with their religious institutes. In particular, we highlight what they like most about their institute as well as the aspects of religious life that have been challenging to them. Where possible, we compare Kenyan responses to those of respondents from the United States as reported by CARA in 2016 (Ngundo and Gautier 2017). We also separate out responses between men and women for clearer comparisons to the data found in other parts of this book.

Characteristics of the Entrance Class of 2017

Background characteristics of the men and women of the entrance class of 2017 in Kenya are presented here with comparisons, where available, to the U.S. respondents from the CARA study of the entrance class of 2016.

Gender

Of the 407 respondents who entered religious life in Kenya in 2017, some 289 were women (71 percent) and 118 were men (29 percent), as seen in figure 8.1. These results suggest that female entrants were more likely than males to participate in this survey, but, in general, Kenya has more religious institutes of women than of men. This fact probably explains why there are more female respondents than male.

Nationality

Overall, more than seven in ten respondents (72 percent) identify as Kenyans. Outside Kenya, Tanzania and Uganda are the most frequently mentioned countries of birth of these new entrants.

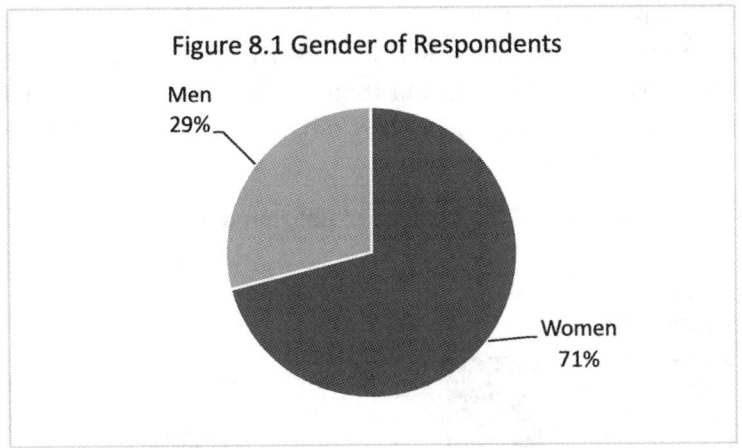

Figure 8.1 Gender of Respondents
Men 29%
Women 71%

Family Religious Background

Regardless of the religious affiliation of their parents, more than seven in ten (72 percent) report that religion was "very important" to their mother when they were growing up. Similarly, half (50 percent) report that religion was "very important" to their father when they were growing up (figure 8.2). These findings show that for the majority of respondents, religion was more likely to be "very important" to their mother than to their father. Other research has also shown that, in general, Kenya has more women than men who profess a religious faith.

The study further sought to establish the Catholic status of their parents at the time they entered religious life. The findings show that a majority of respondents had one or both parents in the Catholic faith at the time they entered. To the question whether father was Catholic at the time of entering religious life, more than eight in ten (83 percent) say yes to this. Similarly, almost all (98 percent) respondents say their mother was Catholic when they entered religious life. The purpose underlying this investigation is the question of one's level of faith. A person who was raised in the Catholic faith will more easily grasp the deeper elements of faith taught in formation, while one raised in a non-Catholic family may need closer attention during their formation process, hence the need to establish the Catholic background of parents.

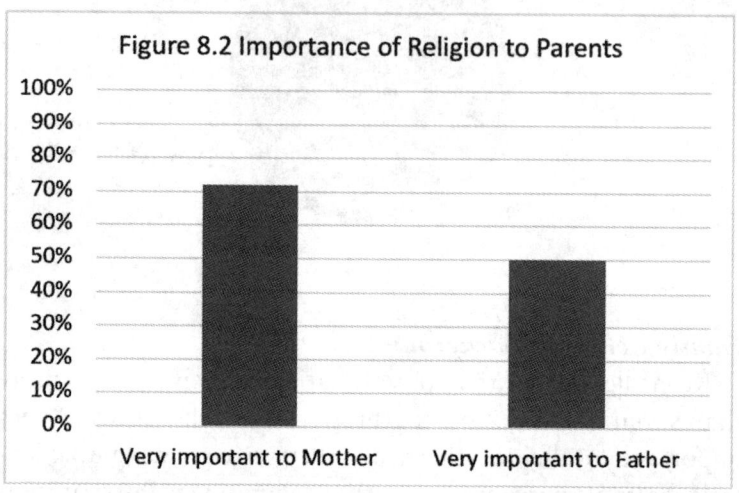

The 2017 study of new entrants in Kenya shows very similar results to the CARA study of new entrants in the United States in 2016, in which eight in ten respondents overall reported that both parents are Catholic (Ngundo 2018). Eight in ten women (79 percent) and just over eight in ten men (83 percent) in the U.S. study reported that both parents were Catholic at the time they were growing up (Ngundo and Gautier 2017:11).

Siblings

One in ten members of the entrance class of 2017 have ten siblings or more (see figure 8.3). Seven in ten have more than three siblings (69 percent). Slightly less than four in ten have four to six siblings (38 percent). Two in ten have between seven and nine siblings (20 percent), two in ten have three siblings or fewer (20 percent), and one in ten have no siblings (11 percent).

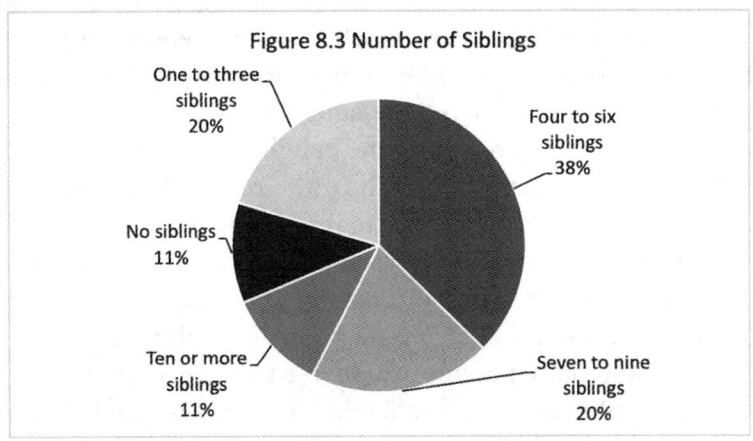

On average, respondents have nine siblings, but 11 percent of the entrance class of 2017 in Kenya report being an only child, meaning they have no siblings. Naturally, people with siblings and those without may manifest different behavior traits. While the one with siblings may be a better team player, a virtue necessary in interpersonal relationships and community living, an only child may tend to be withdrawn and attached to what they have. Knowing these situations may guide the formator to discern the kind of help to offer people with different behaviors arising from their birth situations.

While the most common response to this question is four to nine siblings (58 percent), the most common response in the CARA study was one or two siblings (Ngundo and Gautier 2017:13). This suggests that respondents to the Kenyan study have more siblings than those of the CARA study. Despite economic constraints and changes in cultural beliefs, many African families still value large numbers of children.

Education

Globally, the level of education is one of the main considerations for one to enter a religious institute. In practice, and as a way of promoting vocations, most congregations in Kenya accept high school graduates with a C+ or its equivalent. For Kenyans, this is the minimum university entry grade.[1] Some congregations, however, require candidates to attend some college before entering religious life. In light of this background, overall, slightly more than half of the responding entrance class of 2017 report that the highest education completed before entering religious life was high school or less (52 percent). Just over four in ten report completing some college (43 percent) before entering religious life (table 8.1). After high school, many parents are unable to pay for the college education of their children. While it is true that the Kenyan government provides some subsidy, it is never sufficient.

Table 8.1 What was the highest level of education you completed before you entered religious life?

	Overall %	Women %	Men %
High school or less	52	52	53
Some college	43	43	42
Bachelor's degree	4	4	4
Master's degree	0	0	0
Doctoral degree	0	0	0
Other	1	1	1

Another study, carried out in Kenya by the Centre for Research in Religious Life and Apostolate (CERRA) and the Africa Data Centre that was commissioned by CARA in 2021, presents similar findings about the education level of entrants to religious life (Ngundo et al. 2021). In the 2017/2018 Kenyan study men and women were equally likely to have no more than a high school diploma upon entering their religious institute. By the time of the 2021 study, 56 percent of women and 59 percent of men had a high school diploma or less at

---

1. For Kenyans, these requirements apply to all diocesan seminaries as well as to men and women entering religious life.

entrance (see figure 8.4). For the entrance class of 2021 in Kenya, just 1 percent reports having a postgraduate degree at entrance. The findings show that those entering religious life in Kenya are neither required nor expected to have more than a basic education before entering religious life.

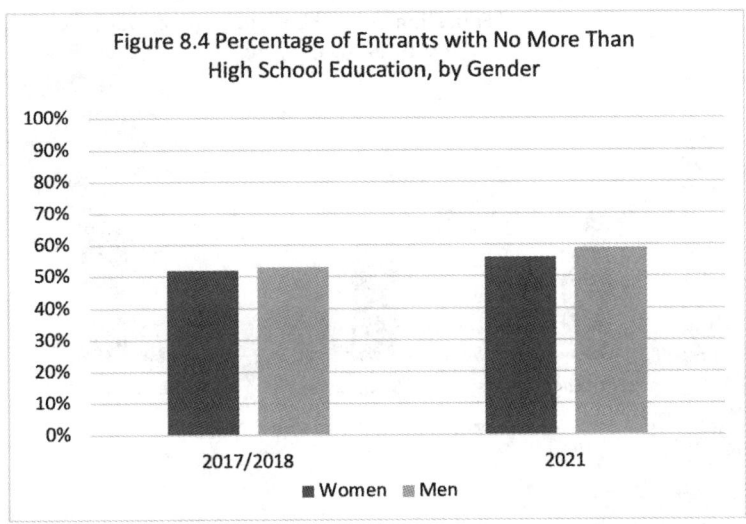

Figure 8.4 Percentage of Entrants with No More Than High School Education, by Gender

This means that the majority of men and women joining religious life in Kenya are more likely than those entering in the United States to have a high school certificate or less. Just 4 percent have achieved a bachelor's degree, the same percentage among both women and men (not shown in the figure). None have gone beyond a bachelor's degree, and a small number (1 percent) have some other education, most likely a technical school diploma (see table 8.1).

Comparing the education levels between the two countries clearly show that those who entered religious life in the United States in 2016 were more educated than those entering religious life in Kenya in 2017 (Figure 8.5). This suggests that those entering religious life in the United States were more likely to have had at least some professional work experience before entering their institute, as compared to their counterparts in Kenya. A CARA special report on women religious in Africa (Ngundo and Wiggins 2017:7) points out the relatively low education levels among African sisters.[2]

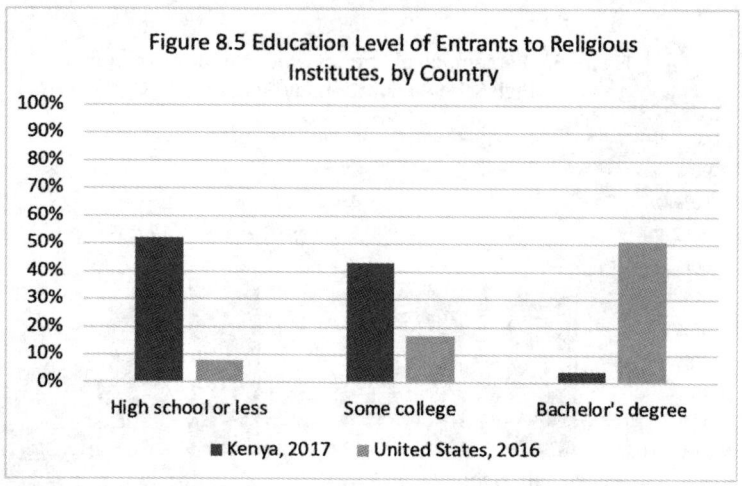

In religious life, education is closely tied to apostolates, which means that those entering religious life in the United States are less likely than those entering in Kenya to require additional training or education before being assigned to challenging apostolates.

2. "Many communities of women religious are still well below the required standard of education to serve effectively in a world that is digital and highly competitive. Towards this effort, the Conrad N. Hilton Foundation has helped to ensure that African women religious are being well prepared to serve the people of God in Africa. ASEC [African Sisters Education Collaborative], through its HESA [Higher Education for Sisters in Africa] program, is doing its best on this whereby many sisters have graduated with Bachelor's and Master's degrees."

Experiences of the Entering Class of 2017 Concerning One's Vocation

Attitudes and experiences of the men and women of the entrance class of 2017 in Kenya relative to their discernment of a vocation are presented here with comparisons, where available, to the U.S. respondents from the CARA study of the entrance class of 2016.

Considering a Vocation to Religious Life

The average age of respondents of the entrance class of 2017 is 28 (Ngundo 2018), identical to their counterparts in the United States as reported by CARA in 2016 (Ngundo and Gautier 2017:10). More than half of the Kenyan respondents first considered a vocation at the age of 15 years or younger (see table 8.2). The minimum age at which one first considered a vocation is 9 while 33 is the maximum age reported.

The youngest respondent of entrance class of 2017 is 18 and the oldest is 47 years of age. Five respondents, who are the youngest child in their family, first considered a vocation at the age of 15, while one respondent, age 47, did so at the age of 10 years.

Table 8.2 Age When First Considered a Vocation to Religious Life

	Overall %	Women %	Men %
15 and younger	53	55	48
Average age	16	16	16
Median age	15	15	16

Men and women are equally likely to have first considered a vocation to religious life at age 16. More women than men, however, first considered a vocation when they were 15 or younger. This is slightly younger than the respondents to the survey in the United States, who were about 18, on average, when they first considered a vocation to religious life.

Attraction to Religious Life in General

The study further inquired about what it was that attracted respondents to religious life. In response, nearly all respondents report that a desire to be of service to the Church attracted them (97 percent). Nine in ten say this desire "very much" attracted them to religious life (table 8.3). About three in four report that a sense of call to religious life (78 percent), a desire for prayer and spiritual growth (76 percent), and a desire to reach out to the poor (72 percent) "very much" attracted them. More than half (52 percent) say that a desire to be part of a community "very much" attracted them.

Table 8.3 How much did the following attract you to religious life?

	"Somewhat or "Very Much" %	"Very Much" Only %
A desire to be of service to the Church	97	89
A sense of call to religious life	90	78
A desire for prayer and spiritual growth	89	76
A desire to reach out to the poor	89	72
A desire to be part of a community	78	52

These findings show some of the positive motivations of a new entrant into religious life. These elements focus on the inner and essential rudiments in religious life. In reality, one should enter religious life in order to devote oneself to the service of God, to prayer and to remain intimate with Our Lord like Mary (Luke 10:39), to reach out to others like Martha did (Luke 10:38), and to share life with others (Acts 2:42-47). These areas are very essential in religious life because a true follower of Christ must be motivated by the desire to grow deeper in virtue as opposed to material inclinations. As can be seen from the table, more than half of the respondents agree "very much" with these elements of religious life.

Attraction to a Particular Religious Institute

Those entering religious life in Kenya in 2017 were asked how much each of several aspects of religious life attracted them to their particular religious institute. Six priority aspects, which more than half of the respondents said attracted them "very much," are shown in table 8.4. The aspects that respondents say "very much" attracted them to their institute include the prayer life of the institute (78 percent), the mission of the institute (68 percent), the life and works of the founder(s) (62 percent), the community life of the institute (59 percent), its fidelity to the Church (59 percent), and its spirituality (50 percent).

Table 8.4 How much did the following attract you to your religious institute?

	"Somewhat" or "Very Much" %	"Very Much" Only %
The prayer life of the institute	90	78
The mission of the institute	89	68
The life and works of the founder(s)	82	62
The community life of the institute	80	59
The institute's fidelity to the Church	88	59
The spirituality of the institute	90	50

The choice of a religious institute is often complicated by individual confusion and indecision. An aspirant once told me that she was attracted to our religious institute by our religious habit. My question to her was, "Suppose the habit that attracted you was withdrawn, what would become of you?" The question about one's attraction to their religious institute is essential in assessing the real motivation for entering religious life.

What Things Do You Like about Your Religious Institute?

New entrants to religious life in Kenya, the entrance class of 2017, were invited to respond in their own words to an open-ended question about what they like most about their religious institute. Among the things that respondents say they like about their present religious institute are its community life and unity among members, the prayer life of the institute, its sense of mission and ministries, and the love, care, hospitality, and concern they show for one another. A few of their comments are summarized here.

Community Life and Unity among Institute Members
Concerning the community life and unity of their institute, new entrants say:

Fraternal living in the community and genuineness of members. Prayer life is one that I like.

The solidarity and the care of one another in the congregation. The spirituality and living together.

I like the community life of the members, their faith sharing, eating together, working together and keeping one another in mind.

Living and working together is what I like about my religious institute. We experience joy as we work and go about our life together.

Prayer and Prayer Life of the Institute
Commenting about prayer and the prayer life of the institute, they say:

I very much like their prayer life. They attend Mass daily and they attend Adoration every time.

Daily celebration of the holy Eucharist and Adoration of the Blessed Sacrament attracted me every time I visited the sisters. Even after joining I am still enjoying what I used to see.

Sense of Mission and Ministries of the Institutes
Respondents also recognize the sense of mission and ministries of the institute as other attractive aspects that they like about their religious institute. Some of their responses include:

I like the pastoral activities in the institute. It specializes in taking care of the sick and the poor. I also feel this is my call.

The best thing about my religious institute is the effort to become good shepherds and preaching the Gospel.

Love, Care, Hospitality, and Concern for One Another

The respondents further note that they like the love, care, hospitality, and concern that their members show to each other. Their comments include:

Love and understanding from members of this institute touches my heart. I like it and pray that it continues as I continue to discern my vocation.

The love and care for all the sisters in the congregation regardless of ages is something good.

They have concern for each other in most cases.

The thing I like in our religious institute is hospitality, love and generosity and the charitable deeds.

What Are Some Challenges You Experience in Your Religious Institute?

New entrants to religious life in Kenya were further invited to share what they find most challenging as members of their institutes. Respondents shared many challenges, including community living, language barrier, adapting to a new way of life, and religious formation, among others. A few of their comments relative to some of these challenges are presented below.

Living Community Life

Concerning the challenges involved in living out community life, respondents say:

Living together in community and understanding people of different cultures is proving to be a challenge.

Community living and cultural diversity is a reality which cannot be ignored. At times people in the formation are treated as though they were angels with no personal needs.

Its community living whereby members are unable to bear with one another's burdens. Conflict is not the best in a community.

Adapting to Religious Life

Some respondents cited issues of adapting to the realities of religious life. Some of their experiences include:

Change of diet and even language from speaking our mother tongue to daily English is not pleasant. Some of us find it difficult to cope.

Lack of proper financial support making the sisters depend much on family and friends.

Some rules in the congregation are very hard to follow. Fixed schedules with no room for dialogue is not interesting. All these are disturbing since we are grownups.

Doing away with my career and following only any mission assigned is something I find challenging.

The institute language is English yet not all of us are English speakers. Communicating with others is difficult.

Conclusion

Religious life is an experience that is quite intricate, and therefore only an individual candidate can best attest to its reality for them. During the Year of Consecrated Life, Pope Francis called on consecrated men and women to strengthen their joyful witness to the Gospel by making sure that they "listen attentively to what the Holy Spirit is saying to the Church today, to implement ever more fully the essential aspects of consecrated life" (Pope Francis 2015:9). Young people entering religious life need to be attentive to the voice of the Holy Spirit in order to make the right decisions for themselves. Their choice of a religious institute must be guided by their own Gospel values as well as the charism and mission of the institute. By so doing, whatever experiences that may follow will never prevail over their informed choices. At times, due to lack of guidance, new entrants join religious life and religious institutes for the wrong motives. Live-in experiences with an actual community of interest to them are the best times for discernment.

9

Reflection on Religious Life and the Future Challenges, Opportunities, and Dreams

Margaret Cartwright
Director, Vocations Ireland

Reading and reflecting on the feedback from the new members of religious institutes in Australia, Canada, the United States, France, the United Kingdom, and Ireland elicits deep within me the need to listen with the ear of the heart. I say this because of the sense of hope that comes from the respondents and my conversations with those currently in formation, recently professed, or ordained. The main attraction to religious life, as articulated by those interested in religious life today, is that this is a response to a call from God. From the ancient desert mothers and fathers of the fourth century to the contemporary religious of today, we have witnessed small cohorts of women and men in every generation choosing to respond to God's call to live a radical witness to the Gospel. Pope Francis reminds us of the necessity of this whole-hearted response in a talk given to laypeople about following the Gospel, saying, "Jesus did not make it easy for His disciples.

He spoke of the radicality with which it was necessary to follow Him" (Pope Francis 2019).

In recent decades, Ireland has experienced a huge shift regarding religion and the faith of its young people. In previous eras, Irish Catholicism was acknowledged as a given and vocations to religious life were common. Now, for young people to celebrate their faith or even to acknowledge it is seen as countercultural. However, there is still a noticeable pull for young people toward prayer and community. Even though the quantity may be down, the quality remains as strong, if not stronger than before (Blohm 2021:21). Research in Ireland by Noelia Molina focuses heavily on the experiences of vowed religious working in vocation ministry and on chaplains and counsellors working with young people. She highlights the importance of the experiential spiritual narrative, speaking of how most of the young people interviewed talk at length about the experience of their own calling from the Spirit. Women and men in formation today or who have been recently professed or ordained have shared their awareness of a personal call from God and are very clear in what they are looking for from religious life. Many relate hearing an actual calling while others report experiencing a "spiritual awakening" and hearing a religious call (Molina 2017). Molina acknowledges that the scope of the research can make it difficult for these stories to be related at sufficient depth, but nevertheless underlines the significance of both the research and the narratives on which it is based.

The women interviewed express this call. A thirty-year-old postulant says she was looking for a life of intimacy with God, to become a loving and whole human being through prayer and community life. Some of what she has experienced already has been a confrontation with herself, challenging at times, but she has experienced a heightened sense of the mystery of God's ways and God's caring, loving, gentle presence. She has found prayer and a growing comfort and familiarity with prayer but has so much more to learn, experience, and grow into. A young, first professed sister shares deeply of her journey from university life to that of living in the monastery where she was looking for an authentic, Christ-centered life. Even though this young woman acknowledges that she grew up in a secularized culture and in a family setting relatively indifferent to the Church, her yearning for religious life came unexpectedly from within—an unanticipated propulsion toward something greater than anything she had experienced or any other type of life she had imagined for herself. The deep sense of prayer that is evident among discerners in Ireland today corresponds to the other findings from the studies in this volume (cf. figure 2.1, tables 3.2, 3.8, 3.10, 3.11, 3.13). This desire for prayer is often mediated through ministry and community. As one formator comments, older women coming to religious life are seeking community and are interested in searching for God with other people. They want to be a part of something bigger than themselves. The modern-day searchers come with generosity of heart and spirit, a willingness to leave a home they have already created, or a way of life that was comfortable and the independence to do as they please. They are genuine seekers.

Most of those in formation in Ireland today are aged between twenty-five and fifty and come from professional backgrounds with impressive academic qualifications and life experiences, yet they do not feel fulfilled in themselves. There is a deep sense of being aware of God in their lives and seeking to put their search for God first. The research in this book also highlights that in the United States the educational standard of entrants is at least at undergraduate level (table 2.5). New religious also come with a very rich life experience. All of this needs to be acknowledged by congregations when developing formation courses.

There appears to be a faith crisis in Ireland more than a vocation crisis. We are very aware of our shadow side, evidenced in the increase in marriage breakdowns, rising suicide rates, and the increase in violence, especially in relation to women. In recent years Ireland, like other Western countries, has undergone huge economic difficulties resulting in homelessness, increased poverty, and insecurity in society. All this comes on top of the legacy of the sexual abuse scandals in the Catholic Church. In contrast to this shadow side is the awareness and interest in social justice issues among our young people today. They are knowledgeable on environmental issues and often have a deep spirituality but not necessarily a deep formation in faith.

During a discussion in a Catholic parish at a post vocation event during Vocation Week, the parish priest raised the issue of Irish teenagers not being well catechized, having sometimes been taught religion at school by teachers who are not themselves practising their faith. Faith is caught, not taught, but if the teachers lack faith and there is little faith in the homes, as is the case in many Irish homes today, this will not happen automatically. The big question, then, surely must be: Where can our young people catch their faith? We are seeing an increase today in the growth of young adult ministry groups such as Youth 2000, Net Ministries, volunteer missionary groups, and other faith-sharing groups. This appears to be where young people are getting much of their support. Net Ministries have reported fifteen vocations to the priesthood and religious life in Ireland over the last couple of years. The majority of those entered priestly ministry, while a few chose religious life. Research carried out by Net Ministries has found that those who have followed a vocation have done so with orders who are perceived as being faithful to the teachings of the Church and wear habits or clerical garb.[1] This also corresponds with the findings of the

---

1. Information received from Tony Foy, Director of Net Ministries, taken from their own records, June 27, 2022.

research in other countries discussed in this book (cf. tables 3.10, 3.13). Vocational seekers of these times seem to have a leaning toward the more traditional approach and practice of the faith, being attracted to outward expressions of faith, and from a cohort of younger people already in some way active in or attached to the order or diocese to which they apply. They register as evangelistic/active in their faith rather than static. The director of Net Ministries noticed that during COVID, their mission became very difficult and challenging, but that there have been more vocations in the last two years from this group.[2]

This group, interviewed by the Net Ministries research, reflects a pattern similar to the way many of those in an older generation began their journey to religious life. The move from a pre–Vatican II Church to post–Vatican II theology was something the older generation grew into through solid theological education and the development of an adult understanding of faith. However, today we see some young people who, while lacking formal faith teaching, are latching on to peer-group evangelistic prayer experiences and finding ways of being church as a way of developing their relationship with God. Without the sound Catholic faith education required for real growth in their understanding of Catholicism, they struggle in their search for an understanding of faith which gives real meaning to their lives. Neither the younger nor the older generations have all the answers, but each generation searches for a deeper understanding of our faith and relationship with the God who calls us.

When we talk about vocation promotion, the question of age is often voiced. Should vocation promotion happen only through colleges, universities, and youth groups? My answer to that is that we should always be promoting vocations. This does not mean being inappropriately intrusive, but simply

---

2. Information received from Tony Foy, June 27, 2022.

through sharing our own story and our own faith in our day-to-day lives. Sometimes a seed is sown through a casual conversation, or through something we have read or seen, or through a kind word or good deed. If we believe that it is God who does the calling, and we are only bridges he uses, then it is important that we create environments for young people to engage in church activities and be given the opportunity to explore what God wants from them.

Chaplaincy departments in schools and universities, and inviting young people to join parish activities and take up roles in the parish, play an important part here, as do religious congregations who offer mission opportunities to young people, whether at home or abroad. These are all key vocation promotion opportunities. An observation from one young woman, already temporarily professed in religious life, speaks of this very important point in relation to her own calling. She relates that, if she had not already had an inner conviction that she might have a religious vocation, she doubts that she would ever have been involved in her parish or university chaplaincy. It was this sense of vocation that in fact propelled her toward the Church. We never know where a seed has been sown or who has sown the seed. Another interesting phenomenon since the pandemic that is occurring here in Ireland is a growing interest in the contemplative vocation. A real thirst for community, silence, and deep prayer has been emerging. This has become apparent from the perspective of those already committed to the contemplative life as well as newer discerners to contemplative living. This corresponds to the cross-national research discussed in this book (cf. tables 3.2, 3.6, 3.11, 3.13).

Fr. Malachy Thompson, OCSO, in his talk on contemplative gifts for an emerging post-COVID world, spoke of how COVID has given us a window into our "old normal" and challenged us to begin again, with community at the heart of our lives. The monastic life is a microcosm of the entire Christian life (Thompson 2022). Quoting Pope Francis, he continues that, whatever our vocations, whatever our location and duties in the world, "growth in holiness is a journey in community, side by side with others" (Pope Francis 2018:141). He also cites Sr. Wendy Beckett, who qualifies the term "vocation" by saying that we need it with the deepest fiber of our being, rather than it simply being one of the many options that we could have chosen. Vocation, therefore, is the hard-wired human desire to seek encounter with our Creator, which is at the root of all Christian life.

New members of religious life in Ireland have shown themselves already to have a good understanding of vocation and are looking for silence and solitude, building deep relationships with God as well as total commitment to God. They are looking for mission, sharing a life in common, growing creatively, and a deep prayer life. These young people are coming from multicultural, multigenerational, and multigeographical backgrounds. They have professional experience in teaching, business, fishing, and farming, to name just a few. Some have moved from apostolic communities seeking a more contemplative way of living. New members come from a very busy world, sometimes with experience in volunteer charity and mission work. They have different cultural and social backgrounds, and some are dealing with various health issues. They also have different perspectives when it comes to Catholic doctrine and religious background. It is obvious to the onlooker that both experienced and newer members are finding new, transforming ways of journeying together, enabling each one to come closer to God, to grow and develop, to be joyful and find an inner freedom to be challenged to live their one wild and precious life through a religious vocation.

When the pandemic took hold and Ireland was told to close its churches, we found ourselves being stripped bare of the very stuff that we had held on to for years. We lost loved ones and could no longer find solace within our church communities. We were forced to change our ways, and vocation ministers had much to ponder upon. We began to ask ourselves what we thought about life, our vocation, our application of the Gospel. Pope Francis even asked what COVID had uncovered for us—had it widened our gaze (Francis and Ivereigh 2020)? COVID has given us the opportunity to reflect on religious life, on vocation, and on the Church. Religious life and the Church today are facing a new vision and new possibilities that are challenging yet full of hope. The synodal process that we are now entering might be the very opportunity that we need to help us with that reflection.

Vocation is like synodality. It is a process, a journey on which many people can help us. Synodality is a new path which gives the Church a new way to lead that is more collaborative. It calls us to become a prophetic community and provides us with a vision, a practice, a process, a reform of structure and new style of leadership for leaders and followers alike. Synodality and vocation share some key attitudes, the most important being faith and trust in God. Listening to one another in a real way and supporting one another on our faith journey is essential for building both synodality and a culture of vocation, as is the humility to know that we are building God's vision for the world, not seeing with our own limited vision. All of this needs to be rooted in prayer, relying on the strength of God, since we are being invited to a level of calling that brings us out of ourselves and into the world of another.

My prayer is that we have the confidence to engage with research, to listen to our younger generation, and to participate in the synodal process in finding what God is calling us to as religious in a new way of being Church. I hope that we can allow others to walk with us on the journey, allowing the "I" to become "us," never forgetting that the Lord is walking with us. Pope Francis invites us to dream, saying, "This is the moment to dream big, to rethink our priorities—what we value, what we want, what we seek—and to commit to act in our daily life on what we have dreamed of. What I hear at this moment is like what Isaiah hears God saying through him: 'Come, let us talk this over. LET US DARE TO DREAM' " (Francis and Ivereigh 2020).

Scripture is the epic story of humanity's emergence from fear to trust. When the research on the "Religious Life: Discerning the Future" project began, the response from Ireland was not as forthcoming as in the other countries, due to the various enquiries and reports into sexual abuse within the Catholic Church in Ireland, which left many religious feeling battered, demonized, and silenced (Simmonds and Calderón 2020:6). Today we see religious striving through their normal everyday life to stay in the boat where Jesus is asleep, trusting him and fighting the urge to suggest that he has forgotten us. The silence of Jesus should not worry us or make us lose hope in him. But neither does the silence make us respond by sleeping also. As St. Benedict says in the prologue of his Rule, "Now therefore, let us finally arise. Now is the hour to rise from sleep." The religious of Ireland are no longer asleep. They have once again taken their place in Ireland's church and are beginning to leave fear behind and to trust.

A recent article in *Catholic Ireland* cites a letter that Sr. Una Agnew, a Sister of St. Louis who is an expert on the poetry of Patrick Kavanagh, wrote to the *Irish Times* on November 1, 2018. This has been one of many articles beginning to surface and to reclaim the voice of religious women in Irish society. A well-known academic, Sr. Una warns that while the "damage done by a few nuns must be acknowledged and repented," it cannot be allowed become the whole story of women religious in Ireland (MacDonald 2018). In her letter to the *Irish Times,* Agnew describes it as a "hopeful sign" that professor Deirdre Raftery, an historian of University College Dublin, "with her positive story about women religious, is given prominence in the press", and that the Jesuit journal *Studies* has dedicated a full edition to "the nuns' story." She stresses that it is healthy for the reputation of all academic work that a "fuller narration" is requested so that "bias might be challenged." She goes on to claim that "context is crucial to authentic research" (Agnew 2018). The researchers from the "Religious Life: Discerning the Future" project acknowledge that they are aware that the small number of interviews from Ireland cannot offer a complete view of religious life for women in that country at present, but it is certainly a much-needed piece of research and one that requires building upon. Having witnessed and listened to our new members since this research was completed, I concur fully with their conclusions. The signs are clear that a more acute appreciation of the culture from which today's applicants are emerging is needed if religious life is to survive and flourish. I believe, as did the contributors to this research, that there is a future for religious life. The experience of Vocations Ireland shows that many people are looking for a radical way of life within intentional communities. I think we will see new types of communities emerge, such as lay and mixed communities, as well as a growth in the contemplative way of life. All of this engenders a great sense of hope for the future.

10

Formation Implications from the Data for Religious Life's Newest Members

Ellen Dauwer, SC
Director, Religious Formation Conference

The insights, feedback, critique, and honest reflections of newer members to religious life from Australia, Canada, France, Ireland, the United Kingdom, and the United States evoke a combination of hope, encouragement, and challenge. The prime reason for this hope is that over 80 percent of the respondents from each of the countries surveyed cite that they were attracted "very much" to religious life as a response to a call from God (figure 2.1). God continues to call men and women to religious life today as He has throughout the ages. While ministry, community, social justice, and a myriad of other attractions also beckon an individual to religious life, at the core is a call from God. This is good news indeed!

A second source of hope is that there appears to be little disillusionment and disappointment expressed by the newer religious who were surveyed. Certainly, all people experience some sense of letdown once the initial "honeymoon" days

193

have passed, but the respondents' clear indications of satisfaction are apparent in both the quantitative and qualitative data. For example, a comparison of the sources of encouragement at the time of inquiry into religious life with the current time showed consistency and even some slight increase over time (figures 2.8, 2.9, 2.10). Those who supported newer religious when they first expressed an interest in religious life continue to support them; even those who were not cited as frequently as sources of support (friends outside the institute) at the time of inquiry were mentioned more frequently after the person entered. A particularly encouraging statistic is that 64 to 75 percent of the respondents state that they receive "very much" support from a formator (figure 2.9).

Third, close to two-thirds or more of these newer members (with the exception of those from France) give high marks to their institutes for their sense of identity, focus on mission, fidelity to the Church, and response to current needs (figure 2.13). A strong majority rate their institutes as "excellent" for opportunities for spiritual and personal growth (figure 2.15). Over 50 percent cite various formation activities of their institutes as "excellent" as well (figure 2.16). This is good news for formators and leaders with formation responsibilities. Perhaps it is related to the retention rates of newer entrants cited in table 2.2.

Clearly there are areas for growth pointed out in the data as well. One is a call for greater efforts by institutes to promote social justice (figure 2.13). The younger entrants to religious life are of a generation that has a strong commitment to social justice (Pew, "Generation Z" 2019). This is a call to all religious institutes and the broader Church. Another area for growth is the perceived need by newer members for more preparation for ministry (figure 2.16). This can appear contradictory as newer members enter religious life with far more education and work experience (table 2.5). However, it appears from respondents' comments that some are assigned to ministries for which they have no training (see table 3.6 and the comments following). A third need is a desire for more satisfying relationships in community (figure 2.14). More comments on community life will follow below.

The demographic data contained in chapter 2 shed light on the backgrounds, experiences, and other characteristics of newer religious; table 2.5 is most critical for formators. It displays, among other information, the previous educational experiences that newer members today bring with them to religious life. At least 80 percent of the women have some postsecondary education. The CARA report for the Perpetual Profession Class of 2020 (Do and Gaunt 2021:4) states that 71 percent of these women entered their institute in the United States with at least an undergraduate degree and that 25 percent had previously earned a graduate degree.

In earlier decades of religious life, most women entered religious life shortly after graduating from high school. Eager to meet the growing demands of Catholic schools for teachers, leaders of institutes sent most out to teach upon completion of the novitiate. They later earned a college degree after many years of summer and Saturday study. In 1954, through the efforts of Sr. Mary Emil Penet, IHM, and others, the Sister Formation Movement was launched in order to ameliorate this situation. It advocated for dedicated years of study for newly professed sisters, rather than the lengthy educational model that was used by most institutes at that time. It established colleges and a well-rounded liberal arts curriculum for them to follow (Kennelly 2009).

Today there is little need to provide undergraduate education for most women entering religious life in the countries represented in this meta-analysis of research, as most come well prepared in a chosen professional area. However, while religious education could be assumed in the past, there is often a lacuna among those entering religious life at this time. Several years ago, Sr. Sandra Schneiders, IHM, called on the

Religious Formation Conference (RFC) to meet the needs of newer religious of today with a program that would prepare them theologically and also provide a community of peers (a cohort) for them (Schneiders 2018). Thus, the Together program of the RFC was birthed. Currently five recently professed women participate in this program. They live together in community, study theology at Catholic Theological Union, and engage in a weekly program of ongoing formation.

In addition to prior education, newer members often bring rich and diverse life experience with them to religious life. Table 2.6 points out that, with the exception of those surveyed from France, over 85 percent of the entrants had had previous work experience; most of it was full-time work. It is important to recognize this reality and to incorporate it into the formative process.

Clearly the candidates in religious life today differ significantly from those for whom formation programs of the past were designed. They are not the recent high school graduate entrants of earlier decades nor the new college graduates who entered in the more recent past. They bring plenty of education and work experience with them and require formation programs that recognize this and build upon it. They do not enter religious life naively nor as *tabula rasa*. The second of Malcolm Knowles's six assumptions about adult learning states that adults need to build on their experiences (Knowles 1972). Today's formation programs should tap into the previous educational and work experiences of those in initial formation. For example, they might have expertise in a topic in the formation curriculum and be able to present a session on it. They might also have the opportunity to assist in an office of the institute. These are but some ways in which principles of adult learning can be incorporated into the educational design in initial and ongoing formation.

Beyond the demographic data contained in chapter 2, there are several other insights from the research that have implications for formation. These include a strong desire for prayer and spirituality among enquirers to religious life, a somewhat weaker attraction to the charism of a religious institute, a preference for larger, mixed-generational communities among newer religious, the perceived lack of preparation of formators, and the need for quality initial formation programs.

In addition to a call from God, another strong attractor to religious life for those surveyed in the research studies is a desire for prayer and spiritual growth (figure 2.1). For past generations, the apostolate tended to be core to the call to religious life. In fact, when I was looking at religious life over forty years ago, my uncle (a diocesan priest) asked my mother why I was interested in religious life. After my mother shared with him my desire to share God-given gifts broadly with God's people, he responded that in his time people entered convents and seminaries to "save souls." In each age, discerners use different vocabulary to articulate the call.

Today there are many ministerial options for young women and men. Therefore, there must be a "more" that religious life offers to them in their discernment. Newer religious seek more than ministry; they are looking for ways in which they can deepen their spirituality and prayer and integrate it with ministry and community. This is demonstrated in several of the sets of responses cited in chapter 2: strong attraction to the spirituality and prayer life of their institute (figure 2.2); the importance of spiritual direction in discerning a call to religious life (figure 2.5); and the influence of prayer life and prayer styles of one's institute (figure 2.7).

In addition to typical content in the initial formation program (e.g., vows, charism and history of the institute, and the history of religious life, social justice, and the Church), it is helpful to include information on various forms of prayer and spiritual practices. Often newer members bring their own tried-and-true methods but experience growth when exposed to others. Learning can also be experiential; this involves integrating and using different styles of prayer and contemplation in the program.

That which attracts a person initially to religious life is not always what keeps one as a religious years later. That which appears attractive at the outset from the outside looking in may often be understood later in a different light. What a discerner to religious life sees on the outside are the externals; later, in the formation process, the internals become more visible. This is especially true in learning about the charism of an institute and, more importantly, in internalizing it and making it one's own. An enquirer, therefore, might not be as attracted to the charism nor the story of the founder and their works initially. Only in time does the new religious learn the deep stories of the institute's founding, its charism, its mission, and its ministries (figure 2.7).

The responses of the newer religious surveyed in the research projects indicated that community is an important attractor both for those looking at religious life and for those who have entered it (figures 2.2, 2.7, 2.14). As stated above, young people are able to find ministry outside of religious life, yet the integration of prayer, ministry, and community life that religious life offers can be the pearl of great price to those who seek it.

Quality community life, though, can be elusive in the formation process. It can be hard to find good communities in which candidates and newly professed religious can live. Oftentimes, an intentional community needs to be established for those in initial formation as well as for those who have professed final vows.

At times, formators and elected leaders seek to place newer religious and those in initial formation in communities that will resemble those in which they will typically live throughout their religious lives. They might deem intentional communities as utopian, impractical, and unnecessary. It seems, though, that nurturing the life and vocation of newer members must give precedence through the provision and/or creation of healthy, life-giving communities. As described in chapter 2, newer members express a desire for larger communities (four to seven members or eight or more) and communities that are intergenerational (figure 2.12 and text between figures 2.11 and 2.12).

Two very concerning obstacles to vocational discernment and entrance are raised in chapter 4. Several respondents refer to the lack of preparation of formators and the absence of a formation program. These are serious issues that need to be addressed before an institute accepts a candidate into initial formation.

Similar to other professional areas, unless one is prepared in a given field, he or she will implement the methodology that they experienced themselves or that they observe from the practice of others. For example, unless a student successfully completes a teacher training program, he/she will teach as he/she was taught. Those who are not trained in the area of formation will tend to form new candidates as they themselves were formed, despite the fact that several decades might have elapsed in the meantime.

There are several short- and long-term formation programs in the United States, Rome, and other locales that prepare one to be a formator, presenting a balance of both theory and skills. They also provide a supportive group of peers with whom the prospective formator can engage over the years. The ForMission program of the Religious Formation Conference, for example, is a two-year, nonresidential program in which participants gather for a weeklong residential session twice a year and then engage in continuous learning at home with their institutes. It uses an "it-takes-a-village" methodology that includes an at-home book group, peer supervision, a variety of reflective processes, and a final project.

In addition to initial formation of formators, ongoing formation is also critical. This can take the form of episodic learning through workshops and webinars as well as more quotidian learning through ongoing reading and reflection. Tending to one's ongoing formation enables the formator to continue to learn and grow, paralleling in some ways the transformative process in which newer members are immersed.

Participation in peer supervision is critical for formators as well. This can take place through individual and/or group supervision. Many groups are now offered online, thanks to pandemic-era Zoom offerings. Supervision provides a supportive atmosphere that enables a formator to share joys and sorrows, frustrations and successes, confusion and insights. Often formators find themselves between the proverbial rock and hard place in their institutes because of their ministry and interaction with newer members. They are privileged to peek a bit more into the future of religious life, but this may, at times, create conflict with elected leaders and members who do not always share the same vision or stand on the same ground as formators. Therefore, the support of peer formators in supervision groups can be invaluable in navigating these waters.

The lack of a formation program for new members is an even more serious concern for institutes. In good conscience, an institute should not accept candidates if there is no formation program for them. Merely dusting off a program from the past is not a tenable solution. There are, though, a few routes an institute and its formators can take.

First of all, much formation takes place in intercommunity programs in the United States. There are several key national hubs: Chicago, St. Louis, San Antonio, New York, and Philadelphia each have programs for novices and/or candidates. Other locales have offerings for those in any phase of initial formation. These intercommunity formation programs may be offered weekly, monthly, or quarterly, and, in addition to quality input and speakers, they provide a supportive community both for those in formation and for their formators.

Another option is federation formation programs. Some federations offer a common novitiate program for their members. Others have programs for those in various phases of formation. Some are beginning to look at centralized formation for all phases for their members. This often can provide a larger community and group of peers for those in initial formation. It also decreases the need to have trained formators and designated sites in each of the federation's institutes.

Some institutes partner with another institute to provide a shared novitiate, especially if there is only one novice in each group. Ideally, there would be some commonality between the charisms of the institutes. In this arrangement, each institute provides a novice director for the shared program.

Recently the Religious Formation Conference instituted an InterCongregational Collaborative Novitiate (ICCN) program for member institutes. Novices spend an academic year in the Chicago-based program and interact with newer religious from many other institutes in the area through participation in programs at Catholic Theological Union and in the Chicago-based intercommunity novitiate (a once-a-week program). Each institute designates an at-home formator who is responsible for formation in their charism. Novices spend time with their institute prior to the nine months in Chicago and following it, to complete a two-year novitiate program.

The ICCN was designed to meet both proactive and reactive objectives. It looks ahead proactively to the future of religious life, which promises to be more inter-congregational and collaborative. On the other hand, the program reacts to current needs by assisting institutes that may not have a prepared formator, a local community or designated space for a novitiate, or an updated program. For institutes that have a novice once every several years, it is difficult to maintain personnel and facilities for a novitiate year. The ICCN, which began with two novices and has grown to six, provides a program, peers, and formators for institutes who may not have them or may be looking for a more collaborative milieu.

God continues to call new members to religious life. They enter their institutes with a strong sense of call and a desire for spiritual growth and healthy life in community as well as ministry. They seek to embody the charism and mission of their institutes by serving the needs of the People of God, nourished and supported by prayer and vowed life in community.

Pope Francis calls the Church and its ministers to creativity (Pope Francis 2020:22). The above examples provide some resources and ideas to meet the formative needs of the newest members and their institutes as they strive to prepare them to live religious life in the twenty-first century and beyond.

11

Conclusion

In these studies of the women entering religious institutes around the world today, certain themes stand out as universal. Primary among them is a strong sense of being called by God to this life. The vast majority of the respondents—of all ages, from all parts of the world—have heard this call. An equally strong and universal motivation is an attraction to prayer and spiritual growth, both generally and as mediated through each respondent's particular institute. Universally cited by at least half of the respondents in every country is the attraction of life in community, even though the respondents also acknowledge its challenges.

These universal themes, however, are filtered through the specific cultural, economic, and demographic circumstances which the women encounter, both in their chosen institute and in the larger society. In North America, Australia, and Western Europe, there are few new entrants to religious institutes, and the median age of the members in most institutes is in the upper seventies or higher. The median age in Mexican institutes is also high, in the low sixties. In addition to the age gap created by these skewed demographics, the decrease or even the complete absence of new entrants affects the way an institute's members view their own future and the future of religious life overall, and the amount of effort they are willing to put into inviting and forming new members. This has been less true of religious institutes in Asia and Africa, although the number of new entrants to institutes in India and in some other parts of Asia also appears to be declining recently. The demographic characteristics of a given institute, or of all the institutes in a country, will therefore influence where—and even if—a woman responds to God's call.

The ethnic composition and class stratification of a given society—two factors which are often interrelated—also influence whether women will be able to respond to the vocational call. Difficulties in accommodating their society's ethnic or class differences are cited by respondents in the United States, Canada, the United Kingdom, India, and Kenya. If these differences are pronounced in the larger society, whole categories of women may be deterred from entering an institute where most of the members are of a different race, ethnic group, or social class than their own. If a woman does enter such an institute, ethnic and class distinctions may also make it difficult for her to remain in her vocation, especially when these distinctions operate at an unconscious or unacknowledged level in the receiving community.

Ethnic diversity may also create more obvious difficulties. Respondents in the Indian and Kenyan studies note that their institutes require all members to learn and speak English as a common means of communication between ethnic groups. This may be more difficult for some members than for others, leading to internal stratification and difficulties in group cohesion. In contrast to ethnic or class diversity within their own society, many institutes in the United States, Australia, and Canada have drawn a significant minority of their new entrants from other countries (Johnson et al. 2019; Johnson, Wittberg, and Gautier 2014:19–20). This creates a different set of cultural differences. In the United States, the older respondents are more likely to welcome this ethnic diversity in their institutes, while the younger respondents are less likely to do so. However, the welcoming attitude of the older sisters may be in theory more than in practice, and the new entrants from another country may still experience difficulties fitting into the institute.

Another factor which mediates vocations to religious institutes—and which is often related to class and ethnicity—is the amount of education available to women in a given society. In the United States, Canada, Western Europe, and Australia, the women who enter religious institutes are highly educated, with 80 percent or more having some postsecondary education. This is less true in countries like India, Mexico, and Kenya. In societies where higher education is available to at least some women, a postsecondary education may come to be expected of all entrants, thus screening out those whose class status has precluded this. At the same time, the women who do have more education will also have more professional opportunities available to them in the larger society and may be less interested in entering a religious institute. Those who do enter may chafe at formation programs that do not take into account their prior educational or professional experience. On the other hand, in countries where education is less available, women may be motivated to enter a religious institute in order to obtain an education rather than from a divine call to a religious vocation. This difficulty is cited in the studies of India and Kenya.

Still another education-related difficulty, cited by respondents in both Western and non-Western societies, is being sufficiently trained for ministry. Basic professional training to staff their institute's ministries adequately is cited as a need by respondents in Kenya and India. In Western countries such as the United States, women entering a religious institute have usually completed their professional training. However, administrative and leadership training, both for internal institute positions and for ministry, is still a strongly felt need among respondents in the United States.

Another factor which influences whether and how women in a given country may hear and heed the call of God to religious life is their larger society's culture and values, which they also have absorbed. In North America and Western Europe before the mid-twentieth century, Catholic culture was largely separate from that of the larger secular society. Families raised their children in this encapsulated Catholic culture and sent them to schools which did the same. Since the schools of that time were primarily staffed by women religious, the children had ample exposure to sisters and to their vocation. Young women who became sisters were esteemed by their families and in their culture. But such all-encompassing Catholic socialization is rare today in Western countries, and in some countries may not occur at all. Far from being culturally valued, entering a religious institute may be disvalued and even considered deviant, especially in countries such as Ireland, where the dynamics of a previously dominant religious culture and its expression in religious life have been called into serious question by the scandal of abuse. The studies in this book all show that women with a Catholic background, both in the family and at school, are more likely to consider a religious vocation than those who grew up without these childhood influences. But this background is becoming increasingly rare in some countries, and the chosen "invisibility" of today's women religious has made meaningful connection with them problematic for many seekers. In addition, ideological polarization in in the United States, Canada, and Western Europe may relegate religion and religious institutions to a reactionary minority only, leading entrants from the "conservative" pole to search for institutes which adhere to a traditionalist form of religious life and closing off women in the "liberal" pole from even considering a religious vocation. The research reported here from Mexico seems to show a similar pattern.

The cultural and economic characteristics of a society may also influence the ways women expect to *live out* their vocational call. The national studies profiled in this book find that respondents from different countries, or from different generational cohorts in the same country, vary in which aspect of religious life they value. Some prioritize ministry or service to those in need; others place greater value on prayer and drawing closer to God. Still others emphasize serving the Church or preserving the traditional model of religious life instead of accommodating to secular culture. Conditions within their countries, such as whether education and health care are serious unmet needs or already provided by the state and whether professional opportunities for women outside of religious life are many, few, or non-existent, may influence whether an institute's members live out their vocational call in ministry to the underserved, in administering large institutions, or in re-evangelizing a largely secularized society. The omnipresence of social media in the lives of youth today may cause younger women to seek out institutes that fulfil their desire for contemplation and prayer.

In addition to shaping *whether and how a woman will respond* to the call of God, the cultural, economic, and demographic factors also influence the *kinds of obstacles* which may prevent women from doing so. Culturally, all of the studies covered in this book except for the Kenya research cite the negative impact of secularism on religious vocation, saying that it increases materialism and individualism among the young. Respondents in the United States and Ireland also mention that modern culture provides many life choices for young people, who have difficulty making a firm commitment to any one of them. Respondents involved in vocation ministry and initial formation also cite potential entrants' immaturity or aspects of their family backgrounds as obstacles to true vocational discernment.

Poor theological catechesis and inadequate formation in prayer are other obstacles mentioned by respondents in the United States, the United Kingdom, and Ireland. These respondents feel that the ability to be silent in prayer is a necessary antidote to the continuous bombardment of electronic stimuli today, and they find that this is extremely difficult for many young women to do, even as they greatly desire it. Negative media depictions of sisters in a given society are also cited: that sisters are obsolete, aging and dying out (United States); that they are cloistered and walled away from the world (France and Mexico); or that they are morally compromised by scandals in their ministries (Ireland). At the same time, new entrants cite positive (even if highly fictionalized) media depictions of sisters as a factor that originally drew them to the religious life—which can cause a different set of problems when they encounter less-than-perfect sisters in daily living.

A country's media can also negatively impact religious vocations by the degree to which they emphasize scandals in the larger Church or portray Church teachings as oppressive to women. The negative impact of Church scandals is mentioned in the studies of Ireland, the United States, and the other Western countries. Church scandals have occurred in India and in various African countries as well, but may not have been sensationalized by the media there to the same extent. In any case, Church scandals are not mentioned in the Indian, Mexican, and Kenyan studies in this book as an obstacle to religious vocations.

A society's larger demographic patterns may also pose an obstacle to vocational discernment, most notably in the declining birth rates of many countries. Families with only one child may be reluctant to encourage a religious vocation for that child. This hesitation is not confined to Western societies; the study of religious vocations in India cites it as well. In contrast, the study from Kenya finds that the families there still have many children, and so may be less likely to object if one of them hears a call to religious life.

As chapters 4 and 5 point out, there are also institute-specific factors which pose obstacles to women discerning a religious vocation. Interview and open-ended questionnaire responses from Australia, the United States, the United Kingdom, Mexico, and India cite inadequate formation programs, overworked or part-time vocation ministers distracted by competing commitments, and poorly trained formators unfamiliar with the culture of young women today as institute defects which pose obstacles to women discerning a vocation.

As with the initial call to a religious vocation and the obstacles to following the call, the *remedies for overcoming these obstacles* also display both commonalities and culturally specific divergences. Universally, formators and vocation ministers recommend that the institutes find and take advantage of more occasions to meet and interact with young women. This is considered essential, both for formators and vocation ministers and also for the sisters as a whole. Otherwise, as Fr. Luis's study of Mexican sisters warns in chapter 6, institutes will not realize how their attitudes, routines, and customs may become an "insurmountable barrier" to attracting the next generation of young women to religious life, or to retaining any who do enter.

Another necessity listed by respondents is for institutes to have a budget for vocations promotion and an individual dedicated to vocation ministry. They also stress the need for all professed members to assume their collective responsibility for fostering vocations. More education for formation directors is also a universally felt need, especially to enable them to understand the culture and desires of younger generations. Education and formation for the new entrants is also cited, especially in the areas of theology and prayer. In the surveys conducted in Western countries, spiritual direction is also a felt need. The U.S. and UK studies note that the role of the clergy in fostering or alienating a call to religious life—by their knowledge or ignorance of it, and by the value they place on it—is also important.

There are national differences, however. The U.S., French, Australian, and Canadian respondents differ in the relative importance they attach to having ministry experiences with institute members prior to entering, as compared to opportunities to live with the sisters. Websites devoted to vocational discernment or a particular religious institute are more likely to be cited as helpful by respondents in the United States (in 2019), the United Kingdom, Canada, and Australia than by respondents in France. Respondents from the different countries also vary in the importance they attach to other types of social media in attracting new members.

In addition, respondents in some countries cite internal difficulties within their institutes that need to be remedied. The Indian study recommends addressing the caste inequalities and divisions that persist in many institutes. The Mexican study urges that sisters there become more familiar with and connected to contemporary culture instead of remaining in a lifestyle of "insoluble strangeness" that outsiders might find hard to understand or value. Several U.S. respondents list the need to establish and/or foster healthy local communities wherein to place and form new entrants, while the UK study shows repeated concern to build intergenerational understanding.

God's call is everywhere: at all times, in all places, within forms and varieties that speak to the spiritual, social, and cultural milieu of each person to whom it is addressed. It is incumbent upon religious institutes today to engage in a mutual dialogue with enquirers and new entrants: displaying and living out the charism they inherited from their founders but also exploring how the spiritual hungers of new generations and new cultures are calling it to change and adaptation. Religious life is one of the most precious gifts which the Spirit has given to the Church; it should be extended as widely as the Spirit intends it.

References

Agnew, Una. "The Nuns' Side of the Story." *Irish Times*, November 1, 2018. https://www.irishtimes.com/opinion/letters/the-nuns-side-of-the-story-1.3681848.

Annuarium Statisticum Ecclesiae (Statistical Yearbook of the Church). Rome: Libreria Editrice Vaticanus, 1970–2019.

Attractivité et évolution de la vie religieuse en France; Synthèse de la phase qualitative. 2016. Conference des religieux et religieuses en France (CORREF).

Bendyna, Mary E., and Mary L. Gautier. *Recent Vocations to Religious Life: A Report for the National Religious Vocation Conference.* Washington, DC: Center for Applied Research in the Apostolate, 2009.

Blohm, Keliah. "Young Adults Seek Prayer and Community." *Horizon: Journal of the National Religious Vocation Conference* (Summer 2021): 21.

Burge, Ryan. "Guest Column: Behind the Steep Decline in Church Attendance among Women." Barna Group: State of the Church, March 4, 2020. https://www.barna.com/changes-behind-the-scenes/.

Bruner, J. *Acts of Meaning.* Cambridge, MA: Harvard University Press, 1990.

Bullivant, Stephen. *Mass Exodus: Catholic Disaffiliation in Britain and America since Vatican II.* New York: Oxford University Press, 2019.

Cardinal Suenens, León José. *Promoción Apostólica de la Religiosa en el Mundo de Hoy.* Bilbao, Spain: Desclée de Brouwer, 1963.

Chase, Susan. "Narrative Inquiry: Multiple Lenses, Approaches, Voices." In *The Sage Handbook of Qualitative Research*, 3rd ed., edited by N. Denzin and Y. Lincoln. Thousand Oaks, CA: Sage Press, 2005.

Clarke, Thomas. "Redeeming Conflict." In *Authority, Community, and Conflict*, edited by Madonna Kolbenschlag. Kansas City: Sheed and Ward, 1986.

Conference of Religious India, 2023. https://crinational.org/national.html.

Congregation for Institutes of Consecrated Life and Societies of Apostolic Life. *New Wine in New Wineskins: The Consecrated Life and Its Ongoing Challenges since Vatican II*. Vatican City: Libreria Editrice Vaticana, 2017.

D'Antonio, William V., Michele Dillon, and Mary L. Gautier. *American Catholics in Transition*. Lanham, MD: Rowman and Littlefield, 2013.

Dean, Kendra Creasy. *Almost Christian: What the Faith of Our Teenagers Is Telling the American Church*. New York: Oxford University Press, 2010.

Diener, Ed, et al. "New Measures of Well-Being." In *Assessing Well-Being, Social Indicators Research Series*, vol. 39. Dordrecht: Springer Press, 2009.

Dixon, Robert, Ruth Webber, Stephen Reid, Richard Rymarz, Julie Martin, and Noel Connolly, SSC. *Understanding Religious Vocation in Australia Today*. Pastoral Research Office, Australian Catholic Bishops Conference. Victoria: Australian Catholic University, 2018.

Do, Thu T., and Thomas P. Gaunt. *Women and Men Professing Perpetual Vows in Religious Life: The Profession Class of 2020*. Washington, DC: Center for Applied Research in the Apostolate, 2021.

Esler, Anthony. "'The Truest Community': Social Generations as Collective Mentalities." *Journal of Political and Military Sociology* 12 (1984): 99–112.

Falcó, Luis Fernando, Brenda Hernández, and Carlos Leyva. *Elder Sisters in Religious Congregations in Mexico: Exploratory and Qualitative Approach*. Mexico: Cruces, 2021.

Finke, Roger, and Rodney Stark. *The Churching of America, 1776–1990*. New Brunswick, NJ: Rutgers University Press, 1992.

Finke, Roger, and Patricia Wittberg. "Organizational Revival from Within: Explaining Revivalism and Reform in the Roman Catholic Church." *Journal for the Scientific Study of Religion* 39 (2000): 154–70.

Gautier, Mary, and Thu Do. *Recent Vocations to Religious Life: A Report for the National Religious Vocation Conference.* Washington, DC: Center for Applied Research in the Apostolate, 2020.
Gilbert, Joanna. "Young People in Search of Religious Vocation." In *A Future Full of Hope?*, edited by Gemma Simmonds. Dublin: Columba Press, 2012.
Gourant, Julien, Agnes Coulombeix, and Ambre Moussut. *L'engagement dans la vie religieuse.* Paris: Opinionway Survey for CORREF, 2015.
Gray, Mark. "Exclusive Analysis: National Catholic Marriage Rate Plummets." *Our Sunday Visitor*, June 26, 2011.
Gray, Mark, and Mary Gautier. *Consideration of Priesthood and Religious Life Among Never-Married U.S. Catholics.* Washington, DC: Center for Applied Research in the Apostolate, 2012.
IMDOSOC (Asociación Mexicana de Doctrina Social Cristiana). "*Creer en México.*" Mexico: Encuesta Nacional de Cultura y Práctica Religiosa, 2014.
Inglehart, Ronald, and Christian Welzel. "Changing Mass Priorities: The Link Between Modernization and Democracy." *Perspectives on Politics* 8, no. 2 (2010).
Johnson, Mary, Patricia Wittberg, and Mary L. Gautier. *New Generations of Catholic Sisters: The Challenge of Diversity.* New York: Oxford University Press, 2014.
Johnson, Mary, Mary Gautier, Patricia Wittberg, and Thu Do. *Migration for Mission: International Catholic Sisters in the United States.* New York: Oxford University Press, 2019.
Kanter, Rosabeth M. *Commitment & Community: Communes and Utopias in Sociological Perspective.* Cambridge, MA: Harvard University Press, 1972.
Kauffman, Christopher J. *Ministry and Meaning: A Religious History of Catholic Health Care in the U.S.* New York: Crossroad, 1995.
Kennelly, Karen M. *The Religious Formation Conference, 1954–2004.* Silver Spring, MD: Religious Formation Conference, 2009.
Knowles, Malcolm S. "Innovations in Teaching Styles and Approaches Based upon Adult Learning." *Journal of Education for Social Work* 8, no. 2 (1972): 32–39.

Kramarek, Michal J., and Mary L. Gautier. *Recent Vocations to Religious Life in Canada: A Report for the National Association of Vocation and Formation Directors.* Washington, DC: Center for Applied Research in the Apostolate, 2018.

Little, Lester K. *Religious Poverty and the Profit Economy in Medieval Europe.* Ithaca, NY: Cornell University Press, 1978.

MacDonald, Sarah. "The Nuns' Side of the Story Must Be Told." *Catholic Ireland*, November 13, 2018. https://www.catholicireland.net/nuns-side-story-must-told/.

Mangion, Carmen M. *Catholic Nuns and Sisters in a Secular Age: Britain, 1945–90.* Manchester, UK: Manchester University Press, 2020.

Mannheim, Karl. "The Problem of Generations." In *Essays on the Sociology of Knowledge*, 276–322. London: Routledge & Kegan Paul, 1952 (1928).

Mbonu, Caroline N. "Reversed Missionary Action: Prospects and Challenges for African Women Religious." *Religious Life Review* (July/August 2016): 217–28.

McCarty, Robert J., and John M. Vitek. *Going, Going, Gone: The Dynamics of Disaffiliation in Young Catholics.* Winona, MN: St. Mary's Press of Minnesota, 2017.

Molina, Noelia. *Religious Vocations in Ireland: Challenges and Opportunities.* Dublin: Vocations Ireland, 2017. https://vocationsireland.com/wp-content/uploads/2019/07/completed-research-doucment.pdf.

Ngundo, Bibiana, and Mary Gautier. *Women and Men Entering Religious Life: The Entrance Class of 2016.* Washington, DC: Center for Applied Research in the Apostolate, 2017.

Ngundo, Bibiana, and Jonathon Wiggins. *Special Report on Women Religious in Africa.* Washington, DC: Center for Applied Research in the Apostolate, 2017.

Ngundo, Bibiana. *Women and Men Entering Religious Life: The Entrance Class of 2017 in Kenya.* Washington, DC: Center for Applied Research in the Apostolate, 2018.

Ngundo, Bibiana, Jeketule Soko, Candida Mukundi, and Ruth Kariuki. *Women and Men Entering Religious Life: The Entrance Class of 2021 in Kenya.* Washington, DC: Center for Applied Research in the Apostolate, 2021.

O'Brien, Susan. *Leaving God for God: The Daughters of Charity of St Vincent de Paul in Britain, 1847–2017*. London: Darton, Longman and Todd, 2017.
O'Donnell, Christopher, OCarm. "Religious in the New Catechism." *Religious Life Review* 33, no. 5 (September/October 1994).
Pew Research Center. "Generation Z Looks a Lot Like Millennials on Key Social and Political Issues." January 17, 2019. https://www.pewresearch.org/social-trends/2019/01/17/generation-z-looks-a-lot-like-millennials-on-key-social-and-political-issues/
Pew Research Center. "In U.S., Decline of Christianity Continues at Rapid Pace." October 17, 2019. https://www.pewresearch.org/religion/2019/10/17/in-u-s-decline-of-christianity-continues-at-rapid-pace/.
Pope Francis. *Witnesses of Joy*. Vatican City: Libreria Editrice Vaticana, 2015.
Pope Francis. *Gaudete et Exsultate*. Vatican, March 19, 2018.
Pope Francis. "Address to Members of the Parish Evangelization Cell System." Vatican, November 18, 2019. https://www.vatican.va/content/francesco/en/speeches/2019/november/documents/papa-francesco_20191118_cellule-evangelizzazione.html.
Pope Francis. *Fratelli Tutti*. Vatican, October 3, 2020.
Pope Francis and Austen Ivereigh. *Let Us Dream: The Path to a Better Future*. New York: Simon and Schuster, 2020.
Rapley, Elizabeth. *The* Dévotes: *Women and Church in Seventeenth-Century France*. Montreal: McGill Queens University Press, 1990.
Rausch, Thomas P., SJ. *Radical Christian Communities*. Collegeville, MN: Liturgical Press, 1990.
Reid, Stephen, Robert Dixon, and Noel Connolly. *See, I Am Doing a New Thing! A report on the 2009 survey of Catholic Religious Institutes in Australia*. Mulgrave, Victoria: John Garratt Publishing, 2010.
Saad, Lydia. "Catholic Church Attendance Resumes Downward Slide." Gallup, 2018. https://news.gallup.com/poll/232226/church-attendance-among-catholics-resumes-downward-slide.aspx.
Schneiders, Sandra M. *Selling All: Commitment, Consecrated Celibacy*. Mahwah, NJ: Paulist Press, 2001.

Schneiders, Sandra M. "Rethinking Religious Formation for the 21st Century." *InFormation* 27, no. 1 (Spring 2018).

Sexton, Catherine, and Gemma Simmonds. *Religious Life Vitality Project: Final Report*, 2015. https://www.academia.edu/41869468/RELIGIOUS_LIFE_VITALITY_PROJECT_FINAL_REPORT.

Siewert, John A., and John A. Kenyon. *Mission Handbook*. Monrovia, CA: MARC, 1993.

Simmonds, Gemma, and Maria Calderón Muñoz. *Religious Life: Discerning the Future*. Margaret Beaufort Institute of Theology, Cambridge University, and the Centre for Catholic Studies, Durham University, 2020. https://www.hiltonfoundation.org/wp-content/uploads/2020/08/Religious-Life-Discerning-the-Future.pdf.

Smith, Christian, Kyle Longest, Jonathan Hill, and Kari Christoffersen. *Young Catholic America: Emerging Adults In, Out of, and Gone from the Church*. New York: Oxford University Press, 2014.

Smith, Sidonie, and Julia Watson. *Reading Autobiography: A Guide for Interpreting Life Narratives*. Minneapolis: University of Minnesota Press, 2001.

Thompson, Malachy, OSCO. "Contemplative Gifts for an Emerging Post-Covid World." Online conference with Vocations Ireland, June 2022.

Turcotte, Paul-André. "Introduction: The Religious Order Today." *Social Compass* 48, no. 2 (June 2001): 163–68.

Turcotte, Paul-André. "The Religious Order as a Cognitive Minority in the Church and in Society." *Social Compass* 48, no. 2 (June 2001): 169–91.

Twenge, Jean M. *Generation Me: Why Today's Young Americans Are More Confident, Assertive, Entitled—and More Miserable than Ever Before*. New York: Atria, 2014.

Wittberg, Patricia. *The Rise and Fall of Catholic Religious Orders*. Albany, NY: SUNY University Press, 1994.

Wittberg, Patricia. *Pathways to Refounding Religious Communities*. Mahwah, NJ: Paulist Press, 1996.

Wittberg, Patricia. *From Piety to Professionalism – and Back?* Lanham, MD: Rowman and Littlefield. 2006.

Index

accompaniment, 98, 115
Africa, 14, 19–20, 174, 204
Africa Data Centre, 172
age gap between newcomers and the established community, 117
Agnew, Sr. Una, Sister of St. Louis, 191
Anglican institutes, 65
Annuarium Statisticum Ecclesiae, 12
Asia, 4, 14, 69, 103, 204
attracting new members, 22, 37, 210. *See* religious life: attraction
Australia, 5, 10–11, 14–23, 25, 32, 35, 37, 42–44, 53, 61, 70, 73, 76–77, 81–82, 89–90, 96–99, 101, 183, 193, 203–05, 209–10

Beckett, Sr. Wendy, 189
bishops, 85
Britain, 103, 111, 131, 137, 211
British National Health Service, 129

Canada, 5, 10–14, 16–17, 19–23, 25, 32, 35, 42–44, 55–56, 61–62, 73, 79, 101, 183, 193, 204–206, 210
canonical vows, 10
CARA, 168, 170–72, 174–75, 195. *See* Center for Applied Research in the Apostolate
Carmelite, 47
catechesis, 128, 134, 207
Catholic faith education, 187
Catholic schools, 18, 85–87, 98, 195
Catholic Theological Union, 196, 201
Center for Applied Research in the Apostolate (CARA), 79, 143, 167–68. *See* CARA
Centre for Research in Religious Life and Apostolate (CERRA), 143, 172
China, 41
Christ, 2–3, 47, 49, 55–56, 58, 66, 71, 101, 109, 111, 118, 126, 136–37, 152, 176, 185
Church sex scandals, 43
class: lower, 69; middle, 69, 119; social, 75,

217

204; stratification, 204; working, 69, 119
community life, 21–22, 26–28, 32, 35, 39, 57–58, 63–64, 68, 73, 113, 117, 119, 125, 137, 177–79, 184, 195, 198
congregational leaders, 106, 125, 128
Conrad N. Hilton Foundation, 133, 174
consecrated life, 44, 128, 139–40, 144–45, 148–49, 152, 164, 180–81
Creer en *México*, 140
cultural coherence or dissonance, 5

dialogue, intergenerational, 132
diocesan priests, 4, 30–31, 88, 197
discernment: 5, 24–25, 27–28, 74, 79–80, 86–87, 95–97, 99–100, 108, 110, 112–16, 134, 149, 175, 181, 197, 199, 207–08, 210
Dominican sisters, 22
Dominican St. Thomas Aquinas, 3

economic characteristics of a society, 206
education: postsecondary, 18, 195, 205; theological education, 187; trained for ministry, 205; undergraduate, 195
education for young girls, ministry of, 3

entering, 12, 18–19, 24, 26, 29–30, 37–38, 42, 44, 50–51, 69, 81, 88, 93, 101, 112, 120, 137, 141, 143–44, 159, 169, 172–76, 190, 195, 203–06, 210
ethnic diversity, 17, 39, 76, 204
ethnicity, 72, 74, 119, 205
Europe, 3–4, 6, 12–15, 44, 103, 203, 205–06
Eucharist, 3, 32, 178
experiences before religious life, 18
evangelization, 3, 14, 152

formation, 5, 12–13, 37–38, 54, 72, 80, 86, 89–91, 94–95, 111, 116, 121–22, 125, 130, 132, 134–35, 141, 144–45, 149, 158–60, 164, 167, 170, 179–80, 183–86, 194, 196–201, 205, 207, 209
formation implications, 193
formation programs, 5–6, 37–38, 90, 121, 141, 164, 196–97, 199, 200–01, 205, 209
ForMission program, 199
France, 5, 10–11, 15–18, 21–24, 29, 32, 34–37, 42–43, 72, 79–80, 82, 87, 99, 101, 193–94, 196, 208, 210
Francis and Clare of Assisi, 109

generations: Generation Me, 132; Generation Z, 43–46,

48–50, 52, 56, 194; John Paul II Generation, 118; Millennial Generation, 46, 48–50, 52, 61–62; Post-Vatican II Generation, 43, 46, 48–50, 52; 56, 61–62, 72; Vatican II Generation, 43, 46, 48–50, 52, 56
generational differences: Australia, 61–65; Canada, 62; France, 72–75; religious life, 41–77; United Kingdom and Ireland, 65–72; United States, 62
generational studies: qualitative, 103, 168, 194; quantitative, 5, 10, 13, 15, 48–49, 168, 194; cross-national meta analysis, 4
global North, 103
global South, 15, 120

health care, 4, 152, 207
history, 1–2, 77, 197
hope: attracted "very much" to religious life, 193; high marks to their institutes, 194; little disillusionment and disappointment expressed by the newer religious, 193

ideological polarization, 206
India, 6, 151–53, 156–57, 159, 162, 165
Inglehart–Welzel Cultural Map, 118
institute leadership, 13–14, 30

institutes of women religious: characteristics, 10, 13,15, 17; generic term, 10. *See* religious institutes
InterCongregational Collaborative Novitiate (ICCN), 201
Ireland, 5–6, 10, 42, 44, 65–67, 70–71, 75, 77

Jesuits, 3–4
Johnson, SNDdeN, Sister Mary, 6

Kanter, Rosabeth Moss, 108, 135
Kavanagh, Patrick, 191
Kenya, 6, 20, 50, 167–77, 179, 204–05, 207–08
Knowles, Malcolm, 196

Latin America, 14, 53, 70, 145
lay missionaries, 4
Latinobarómetro study, 142
leaving, 126, 128–39
LGBTQ+, 96
Lumen Gentium, 1

major superiors, 5, 9–10, 12–15
Mannheim, Karl, 41
members: age, 5, 13–14, 18, 53; aging, 15; born outside the country in which they now serve, 16–17; candidates, 12 , 62, 93, 116, 118–19, 121, 134, 136, 144, 159, 167, 172, 196,

198–200; caring for older members, 14; desire to be of service, 20, 27–28, 51, 176; family characteristics, 12, 17; former sisters, 128; full members, 12–13; initial formation, 12–13, 37, 50, 121, 196–200, 207; leaving, 126, 128–29; married before, 19; mental health, 93, 96, 127, 129–30; nativity, 13; new entrants, 5, 125; newer members, 5, 15–27, 29–39, 47, 76, 91, 95, 117, 137, 155–56, 159, 161, 164–65, 189, 193–200; non-native, 14; novices, 12, 62, 65, 80, 120, 122, 124–25, 130, 134–35, 200–01; older members, 14, 53, 63, 95, 117–18, 127; perpetually professed, 12–14, 17; postulants, 12, 62, 65, 80, 144, 167; retirement age, 14; temporary vows, 12, 63–64; younger members, 45, 55, 58, 63, 115, 136, 155, 162, 165
mendicant orders, 3
Mexico, 6, 139–44, 149, 205–06, 208–09
Molina, Noelia, 184

National Office for Vocation, 107, 113
National Religious Vocation Conference (NRVC), 7, 106

Net Ministries, 186–87
New Measures of Well-Being, 108
New Wine in New Wineskins, 106
North America, 12, 15, 103, 203, 206
nursing sisters, 4

obstacles to vocation discernment, 45, 79–101, 199: absence of a formation program, 199; Church scandals, 84; college debt, 93; external factors, 81–88; fear of commitment, 92; immaturity, 81, 92; institute factors, 88–92; lack of any chance to meet sisters and get to know them, 82; lack of exposure to religious life, 83; lack of preparation of formators, 197, 199; lack of support for vocations from their local diocese or parish, 85; no longer have a strong presence in institutions (e.g., schools, hospitals), 83; not knowing how to pray, 86; poor theological catechesis, 207; public image, 84; secular culture, 2, 81, 123; suggested remedies, 94–100; teachings on sexuality, 84; web presence, 99

pandemic, 188–89, 200
parish, 4, 19, 30–31, 85, 98, 162, 186, 188
Penet, Sr. Mary Emil, IHM, 195
Pope Francis, 181, 183–84, 188–90, 202
popular devotion, 3
prayer life, 21, 26–28, 35, 39, 48, 53, 57, 60, 177–78, 189, 197
Protestant Reformers, 1

Rachel, 138
Raftery, Deirdre, 191
Redemptorists, 4
recommendations for institute practices, 95
religious brothers, 4
religious devotions, 4
Religious Formation Conference (RFC), 193, 196
religious habit, 59, 61, 70, 77, 116, 177
religious institutes: called by God, 203; example of the members, 22, 65; fidelity to the Church and its teachings, 34; generic term, 10; identity, 34, 36, 116–17, 121–23, 129, 134, 139, 194; life in community, 17, 21, 22, 26–28, 32, 35, 39, 49–51, 57–61, 63–77, 90–92; loyalty to the Magisterium, 76; ministries 26, 33, 38, 51–53, 71, 76, 94, 96, 98, 116, 123; personal contact, 24; prayer and spiritual growth, 20, 155, 176–77, 197, 203; promoting social justice, 35; response to the needs of our time, 34; why few women enter, 80. *See* institutes of women religious.
religious life: areas for growth, 194; attraction, 19–23; celibacy, 74; challenges, 58, 67, 104, 109, 118, 120, 125, 137, 153, 155, 165, 179, 183, 203; charism, 22, 26, 47–49, 54, 59–60, 64, 72, 77, 98, 108, 114–15, 118, 136–37; chastity, 75; community life, 21–22, 26–28, 32, 35, 39, 57–58, 63–64, 68, 73, 113, 117, 119, 125, 137, 177–79, 184, 195, 198; decline in the number of young Catholics entering, 44; *embourgeoisement*, 119; encouragement, 22–23, 29–31; founder, 22, 26, 59, 64, 77; integration of prayer, ministry, and community life, 198; living in relationship to others with shared values, 35; ministry, 15, 52, 57, 75; mission, 20, 28, 51, 57, 60, 108; myth, 109, 111, 133; obedience, 58, 64, 74–75, 124, 146; poverty, 74; prayer life, 21, 26–28, 35,

39, 48, 53, 57, 60, 177–78, 189, 197; response to a call from God, 183; rewarding, 56–59, 61–62; spiritual growth, 36, 62, 120, 155
Religious Life: Discerning the Future, 106, 109, 192
Religious Life Vitality Project, 133
religious mystical experience, 3
religious orders, 1–4
religious priests, 4
religious sisters, 22, 103
religious women, total number, 12–13
religious worldviews, 42, 44
retention, 13, 194

Samuel Groups, 131
Scheiber, Carol Schuck, 7
Schneiders, Sr. Sandra, IHM, 195
"second career," 117
Second Vatican Council, 1, 43, 115, 118. *See* Vatican II
Sister Formation Movement, 195
Sisters of Notre Dame de Namur, 7
social justice, 35, 186, 193–94, 197
social media, 93, 95, 99, 135, 163, 207, 210
spiritual hungers, 4, 42, 101, 210
St. Benedict, 191
St. Francis, 3
St. Ignatius of Loyola, 3

Study on Recent Vocations to Religious Life, 106
Synod on Synodality, 160
synodality, 160, 190

Thompson, Fr. Malachy, OCSO, 188
Together program, 196

United Kingdom, 5, 10, 42, 44, 65–71, 77, 79–88, 90–92, 95–96, 99–101, 103, 106, 114, 120, 183, 193, 204, 207, 210
United States, 2, 4–5, 9–11, 14, 16–20, 22, 42–45, 50–51, 56, 59, 61–62, 70, 73, 76–77, 79, 81–94, 96–98, 100–01, 108, 132, 168, 170, 173–75, 183, 185, 193, 195, 199

Vatican II, 49. *See* Second Vatican Council
Vincentians, 4
vocation ministry, 5, 10, 91, 93, 96, 165, 184, 207, 209
vocation promotion, 89, 98, 103, 115, 130, 153, 164–65, 187, 209
Vocation Week, 186

Western Europe, 6, 203
World Day of Consecrated Life, 164
World Health Organization, 129
World Values Survey, 118–19
World Youth Day, 19